Understanding Mortgage Meltdowns

Understanding Mortgage Meltdowns

Arlene V. Carey
Editor

Nova Science Publishers, Inc.
New York

LIBRARY OF CONGRESS CATALOGING-IN-PUBLICATION DATA

Available Upon Request

ISBN: 978-1-60692-789-2

Published by Nova Science Publishers, Inc. ✢ New York

CONTENTS

PREFACE

Borrowers who used alternative mortgages to finance homes during the housing boom have experienced rising foreclosure rates as housing markets have declined.Some types of alternative mortgages may have exacerbated price declines and damaged the finances of consumers and lenders. The use of mortgages with adjustable rates, zero down payment, interest-only, or negative amortization features raise economic risk compared to traditional mortgages. Because some borrowers and lenders did not adequately evaluate these risks, housing finance markets have been hit with significant losses and financial markets have been in turmoil. Alternative mortgages offer some combination of adjustable rates, extremely low down payments, negative amortization, and optional monthly payments. The prudent use of alternative mortgages offers benefits. For example, during periods of exceptionally high interest rates, adjustable rates may suit consumers expecting rates to fall. People whose incomes depend on commission or bonuses may be attracted to mortgages with flexible monthly payments.These benefits come with potential costs for the borrower and for the financial system. Adjustable rates shift the risk of rising interest rates from banks to borrowers. Low down payments increase the risk that borrowers will owe more than their house is worth if prices fall. A borrower owing more than the house is worth may be unable to sell or refinance the house. The use of alternative mortgages in these areas may have contributed to rising defaults and more volatile home prices. More than a trillion dollars of mortgages originated during the boom will reset their monthly payments by 2009.

Chapter 1 - In the midst of the most serious financial crisis in a generation, some claim that deregulation is entirely to blame. This is simply not true and more importantly serves to grossly oversimplify a problem whose roots run deep and involve myriad actors and issues. The simple truth is that many share the blame, and pointing to just one person or organization does a disservice to the American people.

In a time of crisis, the American people cannot afford the same old partisan finger pointing; they need and deserve real, non-partisan oversight. We need a series of hearings that will focus on the root causes and how we can fix a system in order to avoid financial meltdowns in the future. This minority staff analysis attempts to objectively explore the causes of the financial crisis we are in and how companies like Lehman Brothers and AIG contributed to this crisis.

Chapter 2 - Borrowers who used alternative mortgages to finance homes during the housing boom have experienced rising foreclosure rates as housing markets have declined. Some types of alternative mortgages may have exacerbated price declines and damaged the finances of consumers and lenders. The use of mortgages with adjustable rates, zero down payment, interest-only, or negative amortization features raise economic risk compared to traditional mortgages. Because some borrowers and lenders did not adequately evaluate these risks, housing finance markets have been hit with significant losses and financial markets have been in turmoil. Policymakers have responded with a housing rescue package (H.R. 3221 / P.L. 110-289). They have also authorized the Department of Treasury to institute a Troubles Asset Relief Program (TARP) to buy bad debts from banks (H.R. 1424 / P.L. 110-343).

Alternative mortgages offer some combination of adjustable rates, extremely low down payments, negative amortization, and optional monthly payments. The prudent use of alternative mortgages offers benefits. For example, during periods of exceptionally high interest rates, adjustable rates may suit consumers expecting rates to fall. People whose incomes depend on commission or bonuses may be attracted to mortgages with flexible monthly payments.

These benefits come with potential costs for the borrower and for the financial system. Adjustable rates shift the risk of rising interest rates from banks to borrowers. Low down payments increase the risk that borrowers will owe more than their house is worth if prices fall. A borrower owing more than the house is worth may be unable to sell or refinance the house. The use of alternative mortgages in these areas may have contributed to rising defaults and more volatile home prices. More than a trillion dollars of mortgages originated during the boom will reset their monthly payments by 2009.

Using its authority under the Truth in Lending Act (TILA) and Regulation Z, the Federal Reserve issued on July 14, 2008, new rules for mortgage origination. These rules apply to banks and to non-bank lenders. These rules would put some restrictions on the use of prepayment penalties for mortgages with introductory periods and requires disclosures for mortgages with adjustable rates. The House of

Representatives passed a bill to provide additional rules for underwriting practices of alternative mortgages (H.R. 3221) but a similar bill has not as yet passed the Senate.

This report describes alternative mortgages, summarizes recent regulatory actions, and provides an estimate of the geographic concentration of interest rate risk and negative appreciation risk. It will be updated if market developments warrant.

Chapter 3 - On July 26, 2008, Congress passed legislation creating a voluntary program to enable troubled mortgage borrowers and lenders to refinance their loans through the Federal Housing Administration (FHA). Having created the voluntary program, it remains to be seen if people will be willing and able to participate under current financial market conditions. Meanwhile, the pace of foreclosures continues to rise, even as another category of loans, Alt-A, approaches the peak of its payment resets. The foreclosure process may be costly and cumbersome. Some have argued for a moratorium on foreclosures to give distressed borrowers and lenders time to seek financial relief. Others might argue that delaying foreclosures may also delay the recapitalization of the banking system and ultimately delay restoration of stability in financial markets. Proponents might counter that providing additional time to keep current borrowers in their homes will ultimately reduce the magnitude of bank losses and lessen the need for recapitalization.

The persistence of large unsold inventories of housing may be an indicator that house prices may fall further. Further declines in house prices might contribute to more foreclosures and more instability in financial markets. Although economists generally believe that prices adjust to clear shortages and surpluses, it could be argued that the housing market has characteristics that make that process longer and more painful than in some other consumer goods markets. In housing markets, several factors may contribute to a feedback loop (where housing market instability becomes self-reinforcing). Potential obstructions to price adjustment and market clearing in the housing market include builders hesitating to lower prices for new houses because they may have duties to previous customers; the reluctance or inability of some homeowners to sell their houses for less than they owe on their current mortgages; the addition of foreclosures to housing supply when prices fall; the tendency of some potential buyers to wait for market prices to hit bottom; and the reduction of available mortgage credit during a housing market downturn.

A moratorium would have costs and benefits. On the benefit side, it would provide all market participants with more time to assess asset prices and evaluate alternatives. On the cost side, it could delay the ability of markets to clear excess inventories and restore financial stability. Evidence from the Great Depression suggests that states that enacted moratoriums provided relief to some home owners but saw higher costs of credit and fewer loans compared with states that did not. It nevertheless has been argued that natural disasters are an appropriate analogy and that the oncoming schedule of Alt-A mortgage resets creates time pressure that, in the absence of a moratorium, could overwhelm the capacity of loan servicers.

A regulatory foreclosure freeze has been announced by the FDIC for IndyMac loans. Some have called for a foreclosure freeze for loans held by the GSEs in conservatorship. In Congress, H.R. 6076 would set up a deferment period during which home owners would make a payment calculated by formula.

This report will be updated as conditions warrant.

Chapter 4 - As evidenced by the numerous bills introduced in the 110th Congress during the first session, there is much concern over recent developments in the housing and mortgage markets. Bills such as H.R. 3019, the Expand and Preserve Home Ownership Through Counseling Act (Representative Judy Biggert), and H.R. 3666, the Foreclosure Prevention and Home Ownership Protection Act (Representative Betty Sutton et al.), include sections that speak specifically about foreclosures. These bills would authorize studies on current defaults and foreclosures, as well as possible causes. In addition, H.R. 5818, the Neighborhood Stabilization Act of 2008 (Representative Maxine Waters), has been introduced to establish a loan and grant program, administered by the Department of Housing and Urban Development, to help states purchase and rehabilitate foreclosed homes to stabilize as many properties as possible. This report provides a general analysis and overview of current foreclosure issues addressed in the bills cited above.

It begins with a description of the behavior of aggregate foreclosure rates. The behaviors of foreclosure rates are placed in the context of activity in the housing and mortgage market to illustrate any relationships. The foreclosure process is then explained, first from the point of view of a traditional financial lending institution, and then from the viewpoint of securitization when loans are sold in secondary markets. Finally, this report collects information from other studies to obtain an estimate of the average foreclosure costs. A brief discussion of the effect uniform foreclosure legislation may have on costs follows.

Chapter 5 - The U.S. housing market began to slow in early 2006. This downturn has likely played a role in the rise of late mortgage payments and foreclosures occurring across the country over the past year. Many believe that the problem will get worse. The Joint Economic Committee estimates that around 2 million foreclosures of subprime mortgages will occur from the beginning of 2007 to the end of 2009.

As a way to slow the decline, some in Congress have suggested passing legislation that would impose a temporary reduction or freeze in the interest rates of certain mortgages in order to give mortgage market participants, such as borrowers, servicers, lenders, and investors, time to refinance, or otherwise adjust the mortgage terms of borrowers who would not likely be able to keep up with their scheduled payments. Such a measure would modify existing contracts, which would result in the loss of property rights of some individuals in the mortgage market. For this reason, this type of legislation raises some constitutional issues.

This report addresses the possible constitutional implications, most notably regarding the Fifth Amendment's Takings Clause, of a temporary interest rate freeze/reduction as it would relate to investors in mortgage-backed securities (MBSs), which may aid the crafting of such proposals. This report does not seek to address a specific legislative proposal; rather, it merely analyzes interest rate freezes/reductions, generally. MBS investors are chosen for analysis in this report because they likely would be impacted more by such a measure than other potential claimants. However, this is not to suggest that other mortgage market participants could not or would not raise legal challenges because of an interest rate freeze/reduction.

This report presents an overview of Congress's authority, pursuant to the Commerce and Bankruptcy Clauses, to pass laws pertaining to mortgages, and reviews Contract Clause, Substantive Due Process, and Takings Clause jurisprudence. After explaining why Contract Clause and Substantive Due Process claims appear less relevant to the question, this report considers the test a court would likely use in assessing whether a federal interest rate freeze/reduction would offend the Takings Clause, while pointing out that courts could apply a different test in this situation. It also suggests that courts' analyses could vary according to whether they focus on the impact that an interest rate freeze/reduction has on whole MBS trusts or specific investment tranches of those trusts. Where the focus is on tranches of mortgage-backed securitized trusts, a federal interest rate freeze/reduction, in a minority of cases, potentially could be considered a "taking" requiring just compensation for the purpose of the Fifth Amendment. Such a finding would be even less likely where the focus is on the impact to whole trusts. The number of likely successful claims and the overall potential liability of the federal government for those claims (and the litigation costs of unsuccessful claims) is not possible to assess, at least within the scope of this report.

Chapter 6 - Subprime mortgages are loans extended to borrowers with weak credit profiles. Subprime mortgages entail higher risk of delinquency and default. Recent increases in subprime borrower foreclosures and lender bankruptcies have prompted concerns that some lenders' underwriting guidelines are too loose and that some borrowers may not have fully understood the risks of the mortgage products they chose. Regulatory agencies are revisiting the guidance they provide lenders and are reevaluating required disclosures to consumers. In addition, Congress is holding hearings on the subject and may consider consumer protection legislation.

Subprime foreclosures have reached the highs of the 2000-200 1 recession but delinquency rates are not the same across mortgage features. The adjustable interest rate (ARM) feature is currently associated with higher delinquency rates than comparable fixed rate loans. However, the delinquency rate of loans with the negative amortization (NegAm) feature has remained below 1%, the range normally associated with less risky loans. NegAm is a loan that allows a monthly payment less than the current interest on the loan with the remaining interest added to the principal, thus increasing the loan balance.

Financial regulators issued a guidance for alternative mortgage products in October 2006 and issued a proposed statement for subprime lending in March 2007. The guidances require that consumers be given plain-language explanations of the risks of their mortgages. Borrowers must be qualified for mortgage loans based on the ability to repay the loan, not based on speculation about future increases in the value of the real estate collateral. The proposed guidance also seeks to limit payment shock and prepayment penalties. Policymakers are faced with the challenge of balancing the benefits of access to credit against the costs of potential foreclosures.

This report will be updated in the event of significant regulatory or legislative change.

Chapter 7 - This report summarizes and analyzes four previous government market interventions (Home Owners Loan Corporation in 1933, Continental Illinois in 1984, the savings and loan insurance fund shortfall in 1989, and the Latin American debt crisis in 1989), in light of current mortgage market conditions. Current proposals to help delinquent homeowners share many features in common with all of these actions.

The Home Owners Loan Corporation (HOLC) purchased delinquent mortgages at a discount and worked with homeowners to restructure the mortgages into more manageable terms. HOLC accepted slightly more than one million applications from homeowners to refinance their homes between June 1933 and June 1935. It rejected 488,000 applications, most for "inadequate security" and "lack of distress." HOLC foreclosed on 194,000 of those it was attempting to assist. At the time, many had serious concern that HOLC could be a costly undertaking, but when it disbanded in the early 1 950s, HOLC returned a small profit to the government. HOLC successfully conceived and implemented new ways to contact delinquent homeowners and, in some cases, help homeowners find new jobs.

In 1984, Continental Illinois National Bank suffered a run after loans that it had not properly underwritten failed. The Federal Reserve and the Federal Deposit Insurance Corporation led intervention efforts. There were concerns that allowing the bank to fail could have serious repercussions throughout the financial system. This led to the FDIC Improvement Act of 1991.

In the 1980s, the Federal Savings and Loan Insurance Corporation approached insolvency because of the failure of member savings and loan institutions, also known as thrifts. Working together, Congress and the George H. W. Bush administration established the Resolution Trust Corporation (RTC), which was funded by the Resolution Funding Corporation (REFCORP). The thrift industry is still paying off the intervention operation, which is estimated to have cost $152.9 billion.

In 1989, Brady bonds helped less developed countries, mostly in Latin America, restructure their debt by renegotiating terms and writing down some of the loans. The plan, proposed by then-U.S. Treasury Secretary Nicholas F. Brady, overcame coordination problems in previous restructuring efforts. In addition to writing down some loans, the plan included some interest rate reductions, and having debtor nations post U.S. Treasury bonds as collateral with the Federal Reserve. Approximately $91.8 billion was refinanced under the plan. Repayment continues today.

Chapter 8 - Financial markets underwent severe stress during the week of September 15-22, 2008. After Lehman Brothers declared bankruptcy and AIG received a bridge loan from the Federal Reserve, policymakers reassessed their case-by-case approach to resolving financial problems. Secretary of the Treasury Paulson announced a plan to allow Treasury to purchase mortgage-related assets from U.S. financial institutions. The announced intent of the plan is to unclog financial markets, increase the health of the banking sector, and reduce ongoing risks to the economy. This report discusses a draft of the proposal as it stood on September 21, 2008, and analyzes frequently asked questions. This report will be updated as conditions warrant.

In: Understanding Mortgage Meltdowns ISBN: 978-1-60692-789-2
Editor: A. V. Carey

Chapter 1

EXAMINING THE CAUSES OF THE CREDIT CRISIS OF 2008, MINORITY STAFF ANALYSIS, U.S. HOUSE OF REPRESENTATIVES, COMMITTEE ON OVERSIGHT AND GOVERNMENT REFORM*

Tom Davis

EXECUTIVE SUMMARY

In the midst of the most serious financial crisis in a generation, some claim that deregulation is entirely to blame. This is simply not true and more importantly serves to grossly oversimplify a problem whose roots run deep and involve myriad actors and issues. The simple truth is that many share the blame, and pointing to just one person or organization does a disservice to the American people.

In a time of crisis, the American people cannot afford the same old partisan finger pointing; they need and deserve real, non-partisan oversight. We need a series of hearings that will focus on the root causes and how we can fix a system in order to avoid financial meltdowns in the future. This minority staff

* This is an edited, excerpted and augmented edition of a U.S. House of Representatives Publication Examining the Causes of the Credit Crisis of 2008 Minority Staff Analysis.

analysis attempts to objectively explore the causes of the financial crisis we are in and how companies like Lehman Brothers and AIG contributed to this crisis.

The current credit crisis is a complex phenomenon with its roots in a number of places involving a myriad of people and institutions. Key players and institutions include Members of Congress, well-respected members of Republican and Democratic administrations, the Federal Reserve Board, Fannie Mae, Freddie Mac, the Department of Housing and Urban Development (HUD), the Securities and Exchange Commission (SEC), the major private sector credit rating agencies, banks, mortgage brokers, and consumers.

There is no single issue or decision one can trace as a cause of the current financial crisis; rather it was multiple decisions and issues involving many actors over time that led us to where we are today. However, we can point to organizations that contributed greatly to the problem and how their role was the catalyst for others to become involved and eventually fail. Fannie Mae and Freddie Mac fall into this category. They were the central cancer of the mortgage market, which has now metastasized into the current financial crisis. With the help of a loose monetary policy at the Federal Reserve, an overreliance on inaccurate risk assessment and a fractured regulatory system, this cancer spread throughout the financial industry.

A few key elements are critical in understanding how we got to where we are today.

The Role of Fannie Mae and Freddie Mac in Creating the Credit Crisis

If Congress had successfully restructured Fannie Mae and Freddie Mac in 2005 after the Office of Federal Housing Enterprise Oversight (OFHEO) reported on their fraudulent accounting activities, we would likely not be in the crisis we have today. The over $ 1 trillion dollar binge into subprime and mortgage backed securities that Fannie Mae and Freddie Mac embarked upon from 2005 to 2007 would likely not have happened.

By 2005, Federal Reserve Chairman Alan Greenspan was so concerned that he characterized the concentration of systemic risk inherent in the ever-growing portfolios of Fannie and Freddie as, "placing the total financial system of the future at a substantial risk." Recent events have unfortunately proved him right.

The transformation of Fannie Mae and Freddie Mac into the "Affordable Housing Center" was a laudable goal, but to push predatory subprime lending to unspeakable heights and to encourage questionable lending practices believing housing prices would continue to soar was beyond reason. The politicization of Fannie Mae and Freddie Mac over the last decade seriously undermined the credibility of the organizations and prevented their restructuring and reform, with Democrats viewing any attempt at curtailing their behavior as an attempt at curtailing affordable housing. Between 1998 and 2008, Fannie and Freddie combined spent nearly $175 million lobbying Congress, and from 2000 to 2008 their employees contributed nearly $15 million to the campaigns of dozens of Members of Congress on key committees responsible for oversight of Fannie and Freddie. Those who opposed the restructuring of Fannie Mae and Freddie Mac were unwittingly helping to build a house of cards on risky mortgage backed securities.

The motivations for Fannie Mae and Freddie Mac to gamble with taxpayer money on bad nonprime mortgage bets was not entirely a matter of good intentions gone awry. Greed and corruption were unfortunately part of the equation as well. The size and growth of Fannie Mae and Freddie Mac leading up to their collapse were nothing short of astonishing. From 1990 to 2005, Fannie Mae and Freddie Mac grew more than 944% to $1.64 trillion, and their outstanding liabilities grew 980% to $1.51 trillion. These liabilities were equal to 32.8% of the total publicly- held debt of the U.S. Government, which in 2005 stood at $4.6 trillion.

Lehman Brothers, AIG and the Challenges of Statistical Risk Modeling

Lehman Brothers didn't cause this mess but it certainly jumped head first into trying to make money on securitizing mortgage-backed instruments. They followed on the heels of Fannie Mae and Freddie Mac and for precisely the same reasons. If we understand the initial cause of the cancer at Fannie and Freddie, then we can understand how it metastasized to Lehman Brothers, Wachovia, Countrywide, and beyond.

AIG is somewhat different; bad management decisions were made in thinking that the mortgage-backed securities and derivatives could be insured. Yet underlying its bad decisions was the same mistaken reliance on sophisticated but inaccurate computer models, trusting the rating agencies were accurate and that Fannie Mae and Freddie Mac couldn't possibly fail.

Regulation and the Credit Crisis

Democrats are wrong in insisting that de-regulation is the primary cause of the financial crisis. Deregulation is not the problem, rather it is the fractured regulatory system that has banks, investment institutions, mortgage brokers, and insurance companies all being overseen by different and often competing federal and state agencies. The problem is a lack of coherent regulatory oversight that has led mortgage brokers and lending institutions to write questionable loans and investment institutions to play fast and loose with other people's money in purchasing bad mortgage-backed assets.

The words "regulation" and "deregulation" are not absolute goods and evils, nor are they meaningful policy prescriptions. They are political cant used to describe complex policy discussions that defy simplistic categorization. The key to successfully regulating markets is not to either create more or less regulation in an unthinking way. Government needs to design smart regulations that align the incentives of consumers, lenders and borrowers to achieve stable and healthy markets.

Credit Rating Agencies and the Practice of "Rating Shopping"

Some firms that bundled subprime mortgages into securities were engaging in "rating shopping" – picking and choosing among each of the three credit rating agencies in order to find the one willing to give their assets the most favorable rating. Rating agencies willing to inflate their ratings on subprime mortgage- backed securities lobbied Congress to prohibit "notching" – the downgrading of assets that incorporate risky, unrated assets – by their competitors, on the grounds this constituted an anti-competitive practice. Unfortunately, the Republican Congress was swayed by this argument and codified it in law.

MORTGAGE MARKETS: A PRIMER

Prospective homebuyers apply for mortgages from primary market lenders such as banks, thrifts, mortgage companies, credit unions, and online lenders. Primary lenders evaluate borrowers' ability to repay the mortgage based on an assessment of risk that combines such factors as income, assets and past performance in repaying loans. If a borrower does not meet the minimum requirement, the borrower is refused a loan.

Prime mortgages are traditionally the gold standard and go to borrowers with good credit who make down payments and fully document their income and assets. Borrowers with poor credit and/or uncertain income streams represent a higher risk of default for lenders and therefore received subprime loans. Subprime loans have existed for some time but

really took off in popularity around 1995, rising from less than 5% of total new mortgages in 1994 to more than 20% in 2006.[1] Borrowers who fall in between prime and subprime standards who may not be able to fully document their income or provide traditional down payments are sometimes referred to as near-prime borrowers. They generally can apply only for Alternative-A ("Alt-A") mortgages.[2] Starting in 2001, subprime and near-prime mortgages increased dramatically as a proportion of the total mortgage market. These mortgages increased from only 9% of newly originated securitized mortgages in 2001 to 40% in 2006.[3]

Subprime borrowers, in addition to being below the standard risk threshold lenders traditionally deemed creditworthy for mortgages, were increasingly taking advantage of so-called "alternative mortgages" that further increased the risk of default. For example, low- or zero-down payment mortgages permit borrowers who cannot afford the traditional 20% down payment on a house to still receive a loan. Instead some mortgages allow them to pay 10%, 5%, or even 3% of the purchase price of the home. The riskiest loans even allow borrowers to pay no money down at all for 100% financing. Another option is to allow borrowers to take out a "piggyback" or "silent second" loan – a second mortgage to finance the down payment. This is possible because the larger first mortgage means some lenders give borrowers a more favorable rate on the second mortgage. Interest-only mortgages are another alternative type that allows borrowers to for a time pay back only interest and no principal. However, either the duration of the mortgage must be extended or the payments amortize the remaining principal balance over a shorter period of time, increasing the monthly payment, and ultimately the total size of the loan, a borrower will eventually have to repay. Negative amortization mortgages are even riskier, allowing borrowers to pay *less* than the "minimum" monthly interest payment, adding the remaining interest to the loan principal and again increasing the payments and size of the loan.[4]

Adjustable rate mortgages (ARMs) are the most common of the alternative mortgages. ARMs offer a low introductory mortgage rate (the cost of borrowing money for a home loan; it is generally related to the underlying interest rate in the macro economy) which then adjusts in the future by an amount determined by a pre-arranged formula. There are different formulae used to determine the new mortgage rate on an ARM, but in general one can think of these new rates as being related to the performance of the U.S. economy. If interest rates go down during the introductory period of the ARM, the adjusted mortgage rate will be lower, meaning the borrower's monthly payment will go down. If interest rates go up, the borrower's monthly payment will be larger. The prevalence of ARMs as a percentage of the total mortgage market increased dramatically during the housing bubble, from 12% in 2001 to 34% in 2004.[5]

Unlike the above-mentioned alternative mortgages, however, there are sound reasons for borrowers to take out ARMs, under certain macroeconomic conditions. In 1984, for example, 61% of new conventional mortgages were ARMs.[6] However, this was a rational response to the very high interest rates at that time. High interest rates translate into high mortgage rates (the cost of borrowing money). This meant that borrowers at that time were willing to bet that when their mortgage rates adjusted, they were likely to adjust downward due to falling interest rates. This was a sensible bet and one that turned out to be correct.

From 2001 to 2004, however, interest rates were abnormally low because the Federal Reserve led by Chairman Alan Greenspan lowered rates dramatically to pump up the U.S. economy following the attacks of September 11, 2001. Correspondingly, from 2004 to 2006, mortgage rates on 30-year fixed-rate mortgages were around 6%, relatively low by historical standards. Borrowers responding only to these macroeconomic conditions would have been wise to lock in these rates with a traditional 30-year fixed-rate mortgage. The continuing popularity of ARMs, at least until about 2004, relates in part to the abnormally wide disparity between short- and long-term interest rates during this period. Since ARMs tend to follow short-term rates, borrowers could get these mortgages at even lower costs and, as long as they were confident that housing prices would continue to rise, plan on refinancing before their ARMs adjusted upward.[7]

Low short-term rates until 2004 are only part of the puzzle, however. By 2005 short-term interest rates were actually rising faster than long-term rates, yet ARMs remained very popular. By 2006 housing prices had started to slow significantly and yet introductory periods remained popular. In the words of a report by the Congressional Research Service, "The persistence of nontraditional terms could be evidence that some borrowers intended to sell or refinance quickly – one indicator of speculative behavior." However, the report goes on to note that, in addition to speculation, "alternative mortgages were marketed as affordability products to lower income and less sophisticated borrowers during the housing boom."[8] Some other force was clearly at work.

THE ROLE OF FANNIE MAE AND FREDDIE MAC IN CREATING THE CREDIT CRISIS

Successive Congresses and Administrations have used Fannie Mae and Freddie Mac as tools in service to a well-intentioned policy to increase the affordability of housing in the United States. In the process, the U.S. Government created an incentive structure for Fannie and Freddie to facilitate the extension of risky nonprime and alternative mortgages to many borrowers with a questionable ability to pay these loans back. Ultimately, Fannie and Freddie may have purchased or guaranteed up to $1 trillion of risky nonprime mortgages. This, along with a healthy dose of unethical and corrupt behavior by the management of Fannie Mae and Freddie Mac, has contributed perhaps more than any other single factor to the growth of the subprime housing bubble from 2005 to 2007, which in turn was the root cause of the current financial crisis.

In the mortgage market, primary lenders may choose to hold a mortgage until repayment or they may sell it to the secondary mortgage market. If the primary lender sells the mortgage, it can use the proceeds from the sale to make additional loans to other homebuyers. This increase in the funding available to mortgage lenders to lend was the goal behind the creation of Fannie Mae and Freddie Mac.

Prior to the existence of the secondary mortgage market, there was no national U.S. mortgage market. Instead, the mortgage industry was mainly concentrated in urban centers, leaving broad swaths of the country unable to afford home financing. In response, Congress created the Federal National

Mortgage Association, or Fannie Mae, in the National Housing Act of 1934 as a purely public agency. After a number of legislative iterations, Fannie Mae morphed into a private company, a "government- sponsored enterprise" (GSE), with no federal funding by 1970. Congress created the Federal Home Loan Mortgage Corporation, or Freddie Mac, in 1970 to facilitate secondary market trading of conventional mortgages, but in 1989 rechartered it to be a privately-owned corporation to fulfill the same role as Fannie Mae. That purpose was to, "provide capital to primary market mortgage originators in support of an overall federal policy to assure ready availability of financing for housing."[9]

Congress granted Fannie and Freddie certain benefits not available to other private financial institutions. Perhaps most importantly, Fannie Mae and Freddie Mac were able to borrow at rates almost as low as the Federal interest rate, significantly lower than *de facto* non-governmental institutions because investors purchasing Fannie and Freddie's debt believed implicitly (and rightly as it turned out) that the GSEs were backed by the full faith and credit of the U.S. Government due to their origins as government entities.[10]

This was a critical factor in making them very competitive vis-à-vis their private sector rivals, which could not borrow money at such favorable rates. This advantage also had the effect of padding the profit margins of Fannie and Freddie, making them extremely lucrative operations.

1992 was a turning point in the history of Fannie and Freddie. In that year, Congress created a new dual oversight structure for the GSEs. However, it also developed an affordable housing "mandate" for the entities under which Fannie and Freddie were to seek to increase mortgage lending among low and moderate income borrowers. Congress was rightfully concerned that such large corporations with ambiguous ties to the Federal Government and with huge and undiversified investment in residential mortgages presented a significant risk to the American taxpayer if they ever got into financial trouble. Indeed, investors' willingness to buy the companies' debt at such low rates indicates they believed the Federal Government would likely bail them out if they got into trouble. Yet Congress also sought to transform Fannie and Freddie into tools of affordable housing policy.

Thus Congress created the Office of Federal Housing Enterprise Oversight (OFHEO) as an independent entity within the Department of Housing and Urban Development (HUD) to oversee the safety and soundness of the GSEs operations. Specifically, OFHEO was charged with ensuring Fannie and Freddie maintained adequate capital relative to their liabilities and with oversight of their management practices. On the other hand, HUD was charged with setting targets for Fannie and Freddie to lend to low- and moderate- income borrowers. Specifically this meant lending each year had to be meet quotas of families with incomes below the area median income. Additionally, Fannie and Freddie had to demonstrate that a certain percentage of their financing was to families with "low" or "very low" incomes and to businesses in "disadvantaged" localities. HUD would regularly adjust these mission goal targets and was required to evaluate any new initiative on the basis of its support for the affordable housing goals.[11]

How did Fannie and Freddie go about fulfilling their affordable housing mission? First, they purchased mortgages directly and held them in their portfolio. By doing so, they removed these mortgage obligations from the books of primary lenders, whether commercial banks, thrifts, credit unions, or non-bank lenders such as Countrywide Financial. This allowed primary lenders to go about making new mortgages, increasing the availability of funds for all borrowers. The GSEs funded these purchases by issuing bonds and other debt to investors. This was extremely profitable because, as mentioned, Fannie and Freddie could issue debt very cheaply, at rates near the Federal funds rate, giving them a competitive edge over the truly private sector.

Second, Fannie and Freddie engaged in mortgage securitization. Securitization involves taking pools of mortgages and turning them into assets known as Mortgage-Backed Securities (MB S). These securities are then sold to investors such as investment banks and pension funds. They pay investors periodic returns similar to the coupon payments on a bond. MBS also often redirect the interest and principal payments of the underlying mortgages to investors.[12] When an investor purchases a MBS, he is essentially lending money to homebuyers. Securitization is an innovative technique and plays a crucial role in increasing the accessibility and affordability of mortgage lending by connecting homebuyers with the broader financial market as well as by spreading the risk of default more evenly, at least in theory.

Although securitization of mortgages is a valuable innovation, there are risks. If investors are unable to accurately assess the quality of the underlying mortgages, this increases the risk of default and lowers the value of the asset. Therefore, while many private sector, non-bank mortgage lenders were engaged in the packaging of risky nonprime and alternative mortgages into MBS, it was at least believed that Fannie Mae and Freddie Mac had higher standards. However, it now appears that, under political pressure and in pursuit of profit, Fannie Mae and Freddie Mac became increasingly involved in the packaging of risky nonprime mortgages into securities for sale. This did much to fuel the irrational housing bubble and subsequent financial crisis because, as the largest purchasers of mortgages and MBS, Fannie Mae and Freddie Mac exerted tremendous influence on the actions of private sector, non-bank lenders that were underwriting the bulk of the risky nonprime and alternative mortgages which the GSEs would then purchase and market.

Recent analysis of the financial statements of Fannie and Freddie indicates that, contrary to prior assertions by GSE management and their advocates in Congress, both firms were heavily involved in purchasing nonprime mortgages and MBS between 2005 and 2007. Specifically, Fannie Mae and Freddie Mac together apparently held or guaranteed more than $1 trillion in unpaid principal balance on subprime and Alt-A junk mortgages.[13] It now appears that Fannie and Freddie, which had long maintained they operated with high standards for safety and soundness when investing in mortgages, engaged in a verbal sleight of hand in order to dip so deeply into the nonprime mortgage business while maintaining the illusion that they were engaging in low-risk investments. U.S. bank regulators define "subprime" borrowers as those with "damaged credit," to include those with a FICO score of less than 660.[14] However, Fannie and Freddie lowered their bar on the definition of "subprime" and "Alt-A" to FICO scores of 620, dramatically increasing the universe of risky nonprime mortgages they could then purchase and securitize.[15]

Fannie and Freddie did not acquire bad mortgages by accident. Rather, the lowering of their standards for mortgage loans was a steady process drawn out over at least a decade. In 1999, under pressure from the Clinton Administration to increase home ownership rates among low and moderate income borrowers, Fannie Mae CEO Franklin Raines lowered his company's lending standards to include, "individuals whose credit is generally not good enough to qualify for conventional loans."[16] Mr. Raines clearly got the message because by 2004, in joint remarks with Freddie Mac CEO Richard Syron before the Mortgage Bankers Association, he said that they, "made no bones about their interest in buying loans made to borrowers formerly considered the province of nonprime and other niche lenders." Raines went on to say that, "We have to push products and opportunities to people who have lesser credit quality."[17] The GSEs regulator, OFHEO, has also explicitly drawn a connection between the companies and subprime mortgage lending. In testimony before the Senate Banking Committee, OFHEO Director James Lockhart said that Fannie and Freddie purchased and guaranteed, "many more low- documentation, low-verification and non-standard" mortgages in 2006 and 2007 than in the past. He also asserted that the companies did so against the express warnings of his agency. According to Lockhart, about 33% of the GSE's business involved such risky mortgages, up from just 14% in 2005.[18] This reality did little to impinge on Raines' assertions that his company's investments in home mortgages were very nearly "riskless" investments, as he asserted before a Congressional hearing in 2004.[19]

As the largest purchasers and securitizers of mortgages and MBS in the world, Fannie Mae and Freddie Mac exert a powerful influence on the rest of the mortgage lending market. By signaling their willingness to dip ever deeper into the pool of risky subprime and Alt-A mortgages, they created powerful incentives for non-bank lenders like Countrywide Financial and Lehman Brothers to continue scraping the bottom of the mortgage barrel. This fueled the disastrous housing bubble that collapsed with such dire consequences for the U.S. and global financial system.

The motivations for Fannie Mae and Freddie Mac to gamble with taxpayer money on bad nonprime mortgage bets was not entirely a matter of good intentions gone awry, however. Greed and corruption were unfortunately part of the equation as well. The size and growth of Fannie Mae and Freddie Mac leading up to their collapse were nothing short of astonishing. From 1990 to 2005, Fannie Mae and Freddie Mac grew more than 944% to $1.64 trillion and their outstanding liabilities grew 980% to $1.51 trillion. These liabilities were equal to 32.8% of the total publicly-held debt of the U.S. Government, which in 2005 stood at $4.6 trillion.[20]

This phenomenal growth was a function of a very profitable business model that allowed Fannie and Freddie to borrow money cheaply because investors believed (rightly it turned out) that the U.S. Government would never allow the companies to fail and thus gave them low rates of lending. The executives at Fannie and Freddie then invested this money in mortgages and MBS, many of which it turns out were risky nonprime loans. Thus, Fannie and Freddie executives developed a storied tradition of enriching themselves and their private shareholders at taxpayers' expense.

For example, Franklin Raines, Fannie Mae CEO (1998-2003) and former Clinton Administration Budget Director, earned over $90 million during this period. Of that sum, over $52 million was directly tied to achieving profitability targets. In 2003, Fannie's safety and soundness regulator, OFHEO, discovered that Raines and his management team had "manipulated accounting; reaped maximum, undeserved bonuses; and prevented the rest of the world from knowing." OFHEO found that Raines and his team had managed earnings, "to the one-hundredth of a penny to maximize their bonuses while neglecting investments in systems internal controls and risk management."[21] Similarly, Fannie Mae

Vice-Chairwoman and former Clinton Administration Justice Department official Jamie Gorelick earned over $26 million between 1997 and 2003.

This level of executive compensation would not have been possible absent the corrupt use of improper accounting practices by executives at Fannie and Freddie that further padded their salaries and the dividends of their shareholders. In the wake of the Enron and WorldCom accounting scandals, Freddie Mac announced in January 2003 that it was preparing to issue a major revision of its prior financial statements. It turned out that Freddie Mac had been underreporting earnings on derivatives and bonds that had dramatically increased in value due to falling interest rates between 2000 and 2003. Freddie Mac's leadership chose to underreport this income because it sought to protect its image as a sound investment in a stable housing market. Freddie Mac's earnings were eventually revised upward by $5 billion.[22] Then in 2004, OFHEO announced that

Fannie Mae had "deviated from generally accepted accounting principles in order to conceal losses, reduce volatility in reported earnings, present investors with an artificial picture of steadily growing profits, and to meet financial performance targets that triggered the payment of large bonuses" to its executives.[23] The Securities and Exchange Commission (SEC) conducted an independent review of OFHEO's findings and within weeks the leadership team led by Mr. Raines resigned from Fannie Mae. The company's earnings were eventually revised downward by $6.3 billion.

Corrupt practices at Fannie Mae and Freddie Mac extended beyond internal accounting irregularities, however. There also appear to have been inappropriate links between a major private sector mortgage lender and the two GSEs as well. The now defunct Countrywide Financial Corporation was the largest private sector originator and securitizer of mortgages during the height of the housing bubble.[24] As such, Countrywide was in the position of being both a major competitor and a major customer of Fannie Mae and Freddie Mac. Indeed, in July 1999 Fannie Mae and Countrywide entered into a "strategic agreement" under which, "Countrywide agreed to deliver a large portion of Fannie's annual loan volume in exchange for special financing terms."[25] However, this was not the only special arrangement between the two firms.

A federal grand jury in Los Angeles is currently investigating allegations that Countrywide CEO Angelo Mozilo operated a special lending unit called "Friends of Angelo," the sole purpose of which was to provide "VIPs" Countrywide mortgages with preferential rates and lower fees, a perquisite unavailable to the general public. According to 2003 real estate records, Fannie Mae CEO Franklin

Raines received a favorable rate of 5.125% on the first 10 years of a $982,253 refinancing mortgage. Weeks later, Fannie Vice-Chairwoman Jamie Gorelick received a rate of 5% for the first 10 years of a $960,149 refinancing. These loans were around a full point lower than the prevailing 6% mortgage rate at the time. Former Fannie Mae CEO James Johnson (199 1- 1998) also benefited from Mr. Mozilo's largesse, receiving more than $10 million in preferential loans from Countrywide.[26]

ENTER LEHMAN BROTHERS AND COUNTRYWIDE

These sweetheart mortgages fit within a larger picture of relationships among top Democrat Party leaders with ties to the subprime mortgage lending industry. Often, the nexus of Fannie Mae, Countrywide Financial and other firms such as Lehman Brothers involved in packaging and marketing nonprime and alternative mortgages functioned as a revolving door for this mortgage-lending brain trust. For example, immediately prior to assuming his post as Fannie Mae CEO in 1991, James Johnson served as a managing director of Lehman Brothers, the now-defunct investment bank which collapsed under the weight of its bad subprime mortgage bets. After Countrywide Financial, Lehman Brothers was the second-largest marketer of mortgage backed securities during the height of the housing bubble.[27] Similarly, the "Friends of Angelo" program also gave a preferential mortgage to Charles Campion in 2003, who at the time was a lobbyist on the payroll of Fannie Mae and who later left to lobby for Countrywide. Perhaps most disturbingly, Countrywide also singled out Members of Congress with influence over the mortgage-lending sector. Senator Christopher Dodd, the Chairman of the Baking Committee, also is reported to have received a preferential rate of 4.25% for 5 years on a $506,000 loan.[28]

Certainly these questionable lobbying and business practices by leaders of Fannie Mae, Freddie Mac, Countrywide, and Lehman Brothers, can be explained in part by the greed of the individuals in question. However, why would Fannie Mae and Freddie Mac, after years of shying away from the riskiest mortgages and MBS, suddenly plunge headlong into such bad assets in 2005? Following the accounting scandals of 2003-2004, it appears that Fannie Mae and Freddie Mac sought to stave off congressional reform efforts by doubling down on its affordable housing mission that is very popular with key allies in Congress.

Following the revelations about the use of unethical and improper accounting practices by Fannie and Freddie executives, calls for meaningful reform of the two companies became increasingly insistent. In a hearing before the Senate Banking Committee in 2004, Federal Reserve Chairman Alan Greenspan, although previously supportive of the role of Fannie and Freddie in using the innovation of mortgage securitization to provide a secondary mortgage market, expressed his grave concerns about the amount of risk these firms were starting to create for the entire financial system. He correctly identified the ability of Fannie and Freddie to borrow at cheaper rates as an implicit, anticompetitive government subsidy that padded their profit margins by as much as 50% of their total value. This gave the firms an unfair edge over the competition, allowing them to corner over 75% of all single-family home mortgages in the U.S.[29]

> By 2005, Chairman Greenspan was so concerned that he characterized the concentration of systemic risk inherent in the ever-growing portfolios of Fannie and Freddie as, "placing the total financial system of the future at a substantial risk."[30] Chairman Greenspan likely had no idea at the time how soon his prophetic words would come to pass.

Republicans in the Senate Banking Committee led by Senators Hagel, Sununu, Dole, and McCain took up Chairman Greenspan's call in 2005 by introducing reform legislation that would have created new regulatory oversight and limited the size of the portfolios of mortgages and MBS Fannie Mae and Freddie Mac are allowed to hold. While this would not have interfered with their appropriate role in providing a secondary mortgage market, it would have cut into the companies' lucrative profit margins and the salaries and bonuses of their executives. In response, Fannie and Freddie, along with their allies in the homebuilding and realty industries, lobbied Congress hard to oppose the legislation. As a result, the GSE's allies in Congress ensured the legislation was never brought to a vote on the Senate floor.[31] This is incredibly significant, since it is likely that if this legislation was passed, the worst of the housing bubble would have been nipped in the bud, averting the current financial crisis.

Fannie Mae and Freddie Mac have a storied history of lobbying Members of Congress to shield them from regulatory scrutiny. Between 2000 and 2008, their employees contributed nearly $15 million to the campaigns of dozens of Members of Congress on key committees responsible for oversight of Fannie and Freddie.[32] Between 1998 and 2008, Fannie and Freddie combined spent nearly $175 million lobbying Congress.[33] They not only hired lobbyists to influence Congress, they also hired lobbyists to *not* lobby against their interests. These Herculean influence peddling efforts were just part of managing what CEO Franklin Raines referred to as "political risk", or the chance that Congress might in fact take its responsibility to protect the American taxpayers from wanton risk-taking by Fannie and Freddie seriously.

In return, Members of Congress benefited from the efforts of Fannie Mae and Freddie Mac to deliver affordable housing to key constituencies. For example, a press release from key GSE ally Senator Charles Schumer (D-NY) read, "Schumer Announces up to $100 Million Freddie Mac Commitment to Address Fort Drum and Watertown Housing Crunch." A follow-up informed the world that the Senator "urge[ed]" them to "step up" their efforts.[34] If Freddie Mac were truly a private enterprise, it would hardly need "urging" to act on a particular project.[35] The affordable housing mission of Fannie Mae and Freddie Mac is extremely popular with some Members of Congress. For example, at a hearing before the House Financial Services Committee to examine corrupt accounting practices at Fannie and Freddie, Members of the Committee strongly expressed their continuing commitment to providing nonprime and alternative mortgages as tools of the affordable housing policy. These were the same tools that contributed greatly to the housing bubble and financial crisis. For example, Representative Maxine Waters praised the "innovation" of "100% loans" – another term for the risky no down payment alternative mortgages described above. She also advocated that any investigation of corrupt accounting at Freddie and Fannie ought to be limited in such a way "as not to impede their affordable housing mission."[36]

Thus it is perhaps no coincidence that Fannie Mae and Freddie Mac delved more deeply than ever into pools of bad nonprime mortgages in 2005. It was at exactly this time that they were struggling to recover from their accounting scandals and avoid having their lucrative profits reduced by Congressional reform efforts aimed at limiting their portfolios of mortgages and MBS. Yet it was these very portfolios that, according to Alan Greenspan, presented a grave systemic risk to the global financial system. Fannie and Freddie sold their souls to curry favor with key allies in Congress, who blocked reform efforts which, if enacted, would likely have averted the current financial crisis.

THE CHALLENGES OF STATISTICAL MODELING FOR RISK ASSESSMENT

Although Fannie Mae and Freddie Mac bear tremendous responsibility for the current credit crisis, this is a complex problem with other contributing factors. One very significant problem is the difficulty investors have determining the real risk of complex financial instruments such as mortgage backed securities and collateralized debt obligations. Collateralized debt obligations (CDO) are a type of mortgage backed security that creates separate pools of pass-through rates for different classes of bondholders with varying maturities known as tranches, which pay off investors in an order related to the risk level those investors were willing to pay for.[37]

Some of the responsibility lies with the complex econometric models firms use to estimate risk. Lenders and investors rely these days on econometric models to sift large numbers of variables related to risk. These models use statistical methods to assess the likelihood of a given outcome. For example, mortgage lenders use them to rate borrowers' creditworthiness and · the likelihood they will default on a given loan. Buyers and sellers of MBS, CDO, and other assets, such as Lehman Brothers, use them to estimate the underlying risk of these financial instruments. Insurance companies like AIG use them when trying to decide whether to provide insurance for mortgage-backed financial assets based on the likelihood of default.

Statistical modeling is a powerful and innovative tool that has improved the way we live our lives and do business. However, these models are only as good as the quality of their underlying assumptions and the quality of the data plugged into them. They are in essence mathematical machines – data is input and a final product comes out the other side. If the widgets inside the machine are broken, the result will be skewed. And if the inputs are of poor quality, so will be the final product. Incorrect assumptions in the structure of the model and poor data on the asset or outcome being assessed will lead to incorrect decision-making. Despite the sophistication of modern mathematical modeling, the old adage about "garbage in, garbage out" is important to remember.

One particularly egregious assumption made by many in the financial sector who relied on modeling to assess their exposure to risk was that risk itself is evenly distributed. In other words, they believed that risk resembles a coin toss, where on every flip of the coin there is a 50% chance of heads or tails. In fact, markets are incredibly complex and dynamic systems, where seemingly insignificant events in one part of the system can cause disproportionately significant consequences throughout the entire system.[38] The only way to control for such events in designing a statistical model is to anticipate all possible outcomes, and this is essentially impossible. Hence, an over-reliance on modeling without building in appropriate "wiggle room" is unwise. Unfortunately, very few people who use these models to do their daily business understand them completely, and when competition for business in the marketplace is fast and furious, there may seem to be little time to question underlying statisitical assumptions.

Econometric modeling gave many mortgage lenders confidence to dramatically increase the volume of their nonprime lending. Former Federal Reserve Chairman Alan Greenspan has noted that, "where once more-marginal applicants would simply have been denied credit, lenders are now able to quite efficiently judge the risk posed by individual applicants and to price that risk appropriately." At least, this is the theory. However, Greenspan also noted there are concerns about the transparency and completeness of the data being fed into these equations, raising important questions about the ability of lenders and investors to accurately assess risk.[39]

AIG also relied on econometric models when it was trying to decide whether to provide insurance for MBS and CDO packaged by the securities industries, including Lehman Brothers, and fed by the nonprime lending industry including Fannie Mae, Freddie Mac, and Countrywide Financial. AIG provided insurance for these assets using a derivative known as a credit default swap (CDS). Simply explained, this instrument provides its purchaser with a payment in the event that the credit asset (i.e., a MBS or CDO) being insured defaults. AIG had its own internal models, but the accuracy of these models is only as effective as the data provided by the creator of the asset AIG is thinking of insuring – and the originators are relying on their own models. This tiered system of statistical modeling was almost certainly complicated by the extremely proprietary attitude of financial firms toward their econometric models. This is an understandable response when one considers that these models are in fact complex pieces of intellectual property – designing and maintaining econometric models costs these firms a lot of money.[40] However, when viewed at an intellectual distance, piling models upon models and assumptions upon assumptions is the making of a house of cards. Former AIG CEO Robert Willumstad was likely aware of this fact, as the presence of a highlighted trade publication article submitted to the Committee discussing this very problem indicates.[41]

Credit Rating Agencies and the Practice of "Rating Shopping"

Unfortunately, responsibility does not end with statistical modeling. Unscrupulous actors in the financial industry were able to convince Members of Congress and the SEC to insert themselves into the equation by abetting the practice of "rating shopping". Congress' response in the case of "rating shopping" is an example not of "under- regulation", which the heated rhetoric of many in Congress now simplistically blame for the origin of the credit crisis. Instead, it is a case of bad regulation, produced by a Congress that all too often enshrines in law the wishes of special interests seeking their own gain before carefully considering the ramifications of its actions.

Underwriting by commercial banks and credit unions are regulated by the Federal Financial Institutions Examinations Council (FFIEC).[42] Fannie Mae and Freddie Mac are regulated by the Office of Federal Housing Enterprise Oversight (OFHEO)[43]. Non-bank lenders, on the other hand, are often outside the safety and soundness guidance of federal regulators. Between 1997 and 2006, the share of mortgages securitized grew from 49.2% to 67.7%. In dollar terms this was an increase from $423 billion to $2 trillion. Stimulated by the demand of large purchasers of mortgages such as Fannie Mae and Freddie Mac, this growth may have facilitated more lending by institutions not subject to the regulation of federal bank examiners and lowered overall underwriting standards in the mortgage market.[44] The sheer growth potential in securitizing mortgage-backed assets demonstrated by these dollar amounts indicates there was a lot of money to be made up and down the line of this industry.

Assets that bundle these mortgages into mortgage-backed securities and collateralized debt obligations are typically rated by the big three Nationally Recognized Statistical Rating Organizations (NRSRO) – Moody's Corporation, Standard & Poor's, and Fitch Ratings. These firms issue credit ratings recognized by the SEC that provide a signal to potential investors as to the quality of an asset. The ratings of the NRSRO have a tremendous impact on the price an asset can fetch on the market. Typically, a top-level security will be rated by all three agencies, and the rating is generally the same. For example, top-level Aaa/AAA ratings are the same across the three NRSRO 98% of the time. However, for lower-quality assets like subprime MBS rated lower than Aaa/AAA, discrepancies among the three NRSRO may occur almost 50% of the time.[45]

As a result, some firms that securitized nonprime mortgages into MBS and bundled them into CDO were engaging in "rating shopping" shopping these assets at each of the three NRSROs in order to find the agency willing to give the asset the best possible rating. If the bundler didn't like a particular NRSRO's response because he deemed it "too low", he could simply choose to have all or part of the asset rated by the agency willing to provide a favorable rating. However, not having all three NRSROs rate a given security hurts its marketability. A further layer of complexity was introduced when certain tranches of MBS not rated by all three NRSRO were unbundled or combined into another CDO, often after numerous changes in ownership of the asset. When the NRSRO that refused to rate the original security was asked to do so again, the agency would do only with the caveat that it would lower its overall rating of the total security by a few notches. This process is commonly referred to as "notching".

In response to the "notching down" of securities by credit rating agencies seeking to protect their reputation, some in the financial sector sought to change the rules to suit their own ends. According to a paper published by the Federal Reserve Bank of Kansas City:

> "Rating agencies that offered more favorable subprime MBS ratings reportedly lobbied Congress to prohibit notching, complaining that this constituted an anticompetitive practice, and arguing that the dominant players (Moody's and S&P) should instead accept ratings of other agencies without adjustment when rating CDO pools."[46]

Unfortunately, the Republican Congress was swayed by this argument and codified it in law.[47] This prompted the SEC to issue regulations in 2007 prohibiting "notching".[48] It appears that clever lobbyists sold Congress a bill of goods by marketing "anti-notching" regulations as an "anti-competitive" practice.

REGULATION AND THE CREDIT CRISIS

Some in Congress assert that "deregulation" is to blame for the credit crisis, as if "deregulation" is a unified and simple policy prescription that has actual meaning. The words "regulation" and "deregulation" are not absolute goods and evils, nor are they meaningful policy prescriptions. Rather they are usually political cant used to describe complex policy discussions that defy such simplistic categorization. Serious students of economics and organizations understand that the key to successfully regulating markets is not to either create more or less regulation in an unthinking way. Rather, intelligently designed regulations help to *align the incentives* of actors within an organization to achieve some desired end. The organization in question can be a company, a government bureaucracy or even the U.S. economy writ large.[49] If undesired outcomes such as the collapse of credit markets occur, knee-jerk attempts to create new regulations or slash old ones are usually ill-advised and can create unforeseen and unwanted effects down the road. Instead, government needs to design smart regulations that align the incentives actors such as consumers, lenders and borrowers in the economy to achieve stable and healthy markets.

An illustrative example that relates to the credit crisis is the failure of prudential bank regulations to align the financial institutions' incentives with those of the public. During periods of economic growth and increasing asset values, such as the housing bubble, financial leverage always goes up. Leverage is the use of various financial instruments or borrowed capital to increase the potential return on an investment.[50] Banks tend to increase their leverage during economic boom times because it is profitable, and as debt increases so do the risks to investors and the public. Fannie Mae and Freddie Mac are classic examples of this behavior, made all the worse because they were able to borrow even more money than normal because lenders believed rightly that taxpayers were on the hook if Fannie and Freddie collapsed.

Banking regulations require financial institutions to limit their asset risk per unit of capital, but writing regulations that simply mandate an appropriate level is unlikely to work for very long because it is in the interest of bankers to find ways around these requirements in pursuit of profit. For example, banks used the securitization of mortgages to avoid prudential regulations that sought to limit their exposure to risk.[51] Many economists have advocated that government could improve banking regulations by imposing a minimum subordinated debt requirement as part of the capital requirement of banks.[52]

Subordinated debt is a loan or security that ranks below other loans or securities with regard to claims on assets or earnings. In the case of default, creditors with subordinated debt are not paid out until after the senior debtholders are paid in full, making subordinated debt more risky than unsubordinated debt.[53] Financial institutions with a minimum subordinated debt requirement on their balance sheets would be far more cautious about securitizing risky subprime mortgages and other such assets because they would stand to lose money in the case of default.

In 1999, Senator Phil Gramm proposed creating such a minimum subordinated debt requirement to protect taxpayers from institutions such as Fannie Mae and Freddie Mac that used high leverage to turn large profits. He included a requirement in the GrammLeach-Bliley legislation that required the Federal Reserve Board to conduct a study of this proposal.[54] Unfortunately, following intensive lobbying by the commercial banking industry, the Clinton Administration failed to follow up on the Fed's research.[55] This is only one of many examples of possible regulatory improvements Congress could consider. Instead of simply falling back on worn-out tropes like "deregulation", Speaker Pelosi could commit to a top-down review of U.S. financial regulations, seeking to align the incentives of economic actors with the public good with smart regulations. What is not needed is a ham-handed layering of yet more ill-conceived regulations that produces unforeseen and undesirable consequences while limiting the economic growth that produces jobs and wealth.

REFERENCES

[1] Barth, James R., et al., Milken Institute, Perspectives on the Subprime Market 3

[2] DiMartino, Danielle and John V. Duca, "The Rise and Fall of Subprime Mortgages," Insights from the Federal Reserve Bank of Dallas, Vol. 2, No. 11, Nov. 2007.

[3] Tilton, Andrew, "The Subprime Slump and the Housing Market," Goldman Sachs, Feb. 23, 2007 in DiMartino and Duca.

[4] Murphy, Edward Vincent, "Alternative Mortgages: Causes and Policy Implications of Troubled Mortgage Resets in the Subprime and Alt-A Markets," Apr. 18, 2008.

[5] Ibid.

[6] Federal Housing Finance Board, "2006 Mortgage Market Statistical Annual – Vol. 1, p. 17" in Edward Vincent Murphy, "Alternative Mortgages: Causes and Policy Implications of Troubled Mortgage Resets in the Subprime and Alt-A Markets," Apr. 18, 2008.

[7] Ibid.

[8] Ibid.

[9] Weiss, N. Eric and Michael V. Seitzinger, Congressional Research Service, "Fannie Mae and Freddie Mac: A Legal and Policy Overview," Feb. 28, 2008.

[10] Weiss and Seitzinger.
[11] Ibid.
[12] http://www.investopedia.com/terms/m/mbs.asp
[13] Wallison, Peter J. and Charles W. Calomiris, "The Last Trillion-Dollar Commitment," American Enterprise Institute, Sept. 30, 2008.
[14] Office of the Comptroller of the Currency, Federal Reserve Board, Federal Deposit Insurance Corporation, Office of Thrift Supervision, "Expanded Guidance for Subprime Lending Programs," 2001, in Wallison and Calomiris.
[15] Wallison and Calomiris
[16] Holmes, Steven A. "Fannie Mae Eases Credit to Aid Mortgage Lending," The New York Times, Sept. 30, 1999, C2.
[17] Morse, Neil, "Looking for New Customers," Mortgage Banking, Dec. 1, 2004 in Wallison and Calomiris, "The Last Trillion-Dollar Commitment", American Enterprise Institute Financial Services Outlook, Sept. 30, 2008.
[18] Goldfarb, Zachary A., "Affordable-Housing Goals Scaled Back," The Washington Post, Sept. 24, 2008, A11.
[19] Raines, Franklin Delano, testimony before the House Committee on Financial Services, Oct. 6, 2004.
[20] Weiss, N. Eric and Michael V. Seitzinger, "Fannie Mae and Freddie Mac: A Legal and Policy Overview," Congressional Research Service, Feb. 28, 2008.
[21] OFHEO Report, "Fannie Mae Façade," May 23, 2006.
[22] Jickling, Mark, "Accounting and Management Problems at Freddie Mac," Congressional Research Service, Nov. 7, 2007.
[23] Jickling, Mark, "Accounting Problems at Fannie Mae," Congressional Research Service, Dec. 7, 2006.
[24] "The Non-Agency MBS Market Hit an All-Time High," Inside MBS & ABS, Issue 2006, Vol. 2, Jan. 13, 2006.
[25] Simpson, Glenn R., "Countrywide Made Home Loans to Gorelick, Mudd," The Wall Street Journal, Sept. 25, 2008.
[26] Ibid.
[27] "The Non-Agency MBS Market Hit an All-Time High," Inside MBS & ABS, Issue 2006, Vol. 2, Jan. 13, 2006.
[28] Simpson.
[29] Greenspan, Alan, Testimony before the Senate Committee on Banking, Housing, and Urban Affairs, Feb. 24, 2004.

[30] Greenspan, Alan, Testimony before the House Financial Services Committee, Feb. 17, 2005.
[31] Wallison, Peter J., "Regulating Fannie Mae and Freddie Mac: Now It Gets Serious," American Enterprise Institute, May 2005.
[32] Common Cause, "Ask Yourself Why... They Didn't See This Coming," Sept. 24, 2008 in Wallison and Calomiris.
[33] Center for Responsive Politics, "Lobbying: Top Spenders," 2008 in Wallison and Calomiris.
[34] Office of Senator Charles Schumer, "Schumer Announced up to $100 Million Freddie Mac Commitment to Address Fort Drum and Watertown Housing Crunch," Nov. 20, 2006 in Wallison and Calomiris.
[35] Wallison and Calomiris.
[36] Video footage of House Financial Services Committee hearing, accessed at http://www.youtube.com/watch?v=hN31-nKndg8
[37] Investopedia, http://www.investopedia.com/terms/c/cmo.asp
[38] Rickards, James G., "A Mountain, Overlooked: How risk modeling failed Wall St. and Washington," The Washington Post, Oct. 2, 2008.
[39] Greenspan, Alan, Remarks at the Federal Reserve System's Fourth Annual Community Affairs Research Conference, Washington , D.C., April 8, 2005.
[40] Document provided by AIG responsive to Committee request, bates HHOGR000 14473.
[41] Ibid.
[42] The FFIEC consists of: Board of Governors of the Federal Reserve System (FRB), Federal Deposit Insurance Corporation (FDIC), National Credit Union Administration (NCUA), Office of the Comptroller of the Currency (OCC), and the Office of Thrift Supervision (OTS).
[43] OFHEO and the Federal Housing Finance Board (FHLBoard) will be replaced by a new, unitary Federal Housing Finance Agency (FHFA) on July 30, 2009 pursuant to P.L. 110-289.
[44] Murphy, Edward Vincent, Congressional Research Service, "Securitization and Federal Regulation of Mortgages for Safety and Soundness," Sept. 17, 2007.
[45] Calomiris, Charles W., Letter to Nancy M. Morris, Secretary, Securities and Exchange Commission, May 4, 2007.
[46] Calomiris, Charles W., "The Subprime Turmoil: What's Old, What's New, and What's Next," Oct. 1, 2008 (updated version provided by the author).

[47] Cf. P.L. 109-291, "Credit Rating Agency Duopoly Relief Act of 2006".
[48] Speech by SEC Staff: Remarks Before the SEC Open Meeting: Final Rules Implementing the Credit Rating Agency Reform Act of 2006, May 27, 2007.
[49] For a comprehensive discussion of organizational theory cf. Olson, Mancur, The Logic of Collective Action, Public Goods and the Theory of Groups, Cambridge, MA: Harvard University Press, 1971.
[50] Investopedia.
[51] Calomiris, "The Subprime Turmoil".
[52] Shadow Financial Regulatory Committee, Reforming Bank Capital Regulation, AEI Press, 2000 in Calomiris, "The Subprime Turmoil".
[53] Investopedia.
[54] Cf. P.L. 106-102, Sec. 108.
[55] Calomiris, "The Subprime Turmoil".

In: Understanding Mortgage Meltdowns
Editor: A. V. Carey
ISBN: 978-1-60692-789-2

Chapter 2

ALTERNATIVE MORTGAGES: CAUSES AND POLICY IMPLICATIONS OF TROUBLED MORTGAGE RESETS IN THE SUBPRIME AND ALT-A MARKETS*

Edward V. Murphy

ABSTRACT

Borrowers who used alternative mortgages to finance homes during the housing boom have experienced rising foreclosure rates as housing markets have declined. Some types of alternative mortgages may have exacerbated price declines and damaged the finances of consumers and lenders. The use of mortgages with adjustable rates, zero down payment, interest-only, or negative amortization features raise economic risk compared to traditional mortgages. Because some borrowers and lenders did not adequately evaluate these risks, housing finance markets have been hit with significant losses and financial markets have been in turmoil. Policymakers have responded with a housing rescue package (H.R. 3221 / P.L. 110-289). They have also authorized the Department of Treasury to institute a Troubles Asset Relief Program (TARP) to buy bad debts from banks (H.R. 1424 / P.L. 110-343).

Alternative mortgages offer some combination of adjustable rates, extremely low down payments, negative amortization, and optional monthly

* This is an edited, excerpted and augmented edition of a Congressional Research Service Publication RL33775, dated October 8, 2008.

payments. The prudent use of alternative mortgages offers benefits. For example, during periods of exceptionally high interest rates, adjustable rates may suit consumers expecting rates to fall. People whose incomes depend on commission or bonuses may be attracted to mortgages with flexible monthly payments.

These benefits come with potential costs for the borrower and for the financial system. Adjustable rates shift the risk of rising interest rates from banks to borrowers. Low down payments increase the risk that borrowers will owe more than their house is worth if prices fall. A borrower owing more than the house is worth may be unable to sell or refinance the house. The use of alternative mortgages in these areas may have contributed to rising defaults and more volatile home prices. More than a trillion dollars of mortgages originated during the boom will reset their monthly payments by 2009.

Using its authority under the Truth in Lending Act (TILA) and Regulation Z, the Federal Reserve issued on July 14, 2008, new rules for mortgage origination. These rules apply to banks and to non-bank lenders. These rules would put some restrictions on the use of prepayment penalties for mortgages with introductory periods and requires disclosures for mortgages with adjustable rates. The House of Representatives passed a bill to provide additional rules for underwriting practices of alternative mortgages (H.R. 3221) but a similar bill has not as yet passed the Senate.

This report describes alternative mortgages, summarizes recent regulatory actions, and provides an estimate of the geographic concentration of interest rate risk and negative appreciation risk. It will be updated if market developments warrant.

BACKGROUND

More than a trillion dollars of mortgages will have payment resets in 2007-2009.[1] A newspaper account of one resident of Garden Grove, California, illustrates the problem. His monthly mortgage payment doubled and he learned that he owes more than his house is worth because prices of neighboring houses fell by $140,000.[2] It will be a struggle to maintain the higher payments on his resetting mortgage and it is difficult to refinance while he is upside down.[3] The Federal Reserve issued new rules pursuant to the Truth in Lending Act (TILA) to help potential home buyers understand the risks in alternative mortgages and to ensure that lenders follow safe and sound practices. Unlike a regulatory guidance, Regulation Z applies to banks and to non-bank lenders that operate in the subprime and Alt-A mortgage sectors.[4] Mortgage delinquencies and foreclosures are rising and the prospect of coming mortgage resets in declining housing markets suggests that defaults will rise even higher.

Alternative mortgages are sometimes called nontraditional mortgages or exotic mortgages. Alternative mortgages have some combination of variable interest rates, extremely low down payments, interest-only periods, and/or negative amortization. (Amortization refers to the gradual payment of the loan's principal.) In some cases, borrowers intended to refinance these loans or sell the houses relatively quickly. The potential advantages of alternative features for these buyers often depended on the expected path of interest rates and home appreciation. Significant disadvantages became apparent, however, when interest rates and appreciation took what to some was an unexpected turn. The sudden decrease in house price appreciation during 2006-2008 has caused problems for borrowers using alternative mortgages with resets that are expected to occur in coming months.

House prices boomed from 2000 to 2005 in many parts of the country and then suddenly ground to a halt in 2006. Since 2006, house prices have fallen in many markets. Although adjustable rate mortgages are not new, their increased use during the boom was counterintuitive to many economists because mortgage rates were already low by historic standards. Other alternative features were not new but their use by the general public increased during the boom. The increased use of alternative mortgages by unsophisticated borrowers may have been a significant contributor to the rise in mortgage delinquencies and foreclosures.

This report recounts recent events that led to increased foreclosures and the forecast of higher foreclosures, explains salient features of alternative mortgages, summarizes federal agency response, places the potential benefits and risks to consumers and financial systems in the context of economic conditions, and assesses the estimates geographic impact.

EVENTS THAT LED TO UNSUSTAINABLE MORTGAGES

Size and Timing of the Upcoming Mortgage Resets

Mortgage defaults are rising and are expected to increase significantly. Housing prices have slowed or declined in previously booming areas, and it is taking longer to sell homes; troubled borrowers now find it more difficult to sell their property to avoid foreclosure. Many borrowers took out loans with introductory periods that will expire resulting in higher payments even if interest rates are low, and the underwriting of these loans appears to be relatively weak. The combination of mortgage payment resets and weaker housing markets could lead to even higher mortgage defaults in coming years.

There are two periods of higher scheduled resets. Figure 1 shows that the first period (January 2007 - September 2008) had a high proportion of subprime loans. Month 1 in Figure 1 represents January of 2007; therefore, month 23 represents November 2008, which has a low number of subprime resets. After November 2008, the number of payment resets in the Alt-A and option ARM categories increases. Alt-A loans are typically loans that would be considered low risk if everything in the loan documentation turns out to be accurate; that is, the loan has an alternative way to meet “A” standards, such as reduced income documentation. Informally, these loans are sometimes referred to as “liar loans” because of the potential for fraud. An option ARM is a loan that allows the borrower several options for any given month’s payment, including paying less than the current interest due. If the borrower pays less than current interest due then the loan negatively amortizes — the balance increases and future payments rise.

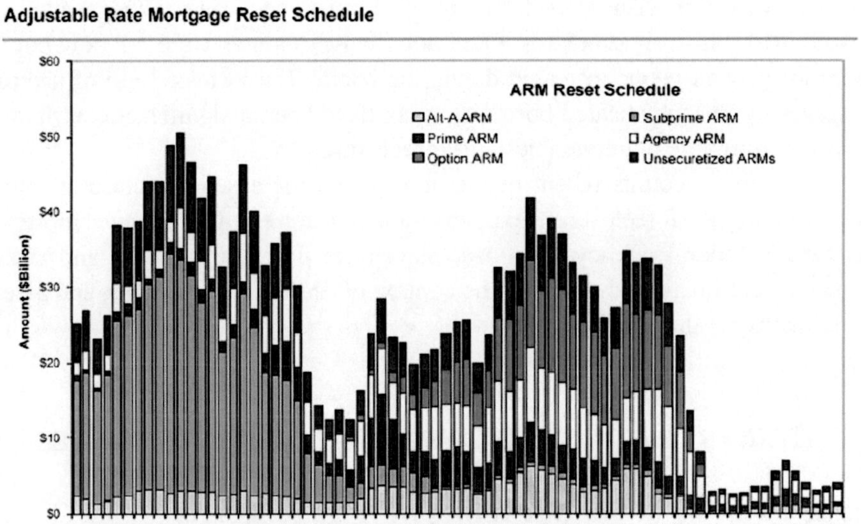

Note: Data as of January 2007.
Source: Credit Suisse Fixed Income U.S. Mortgage Strategy.

Figure 1. Alternative Mortgage Resets.

Interest rates in 2004 through 2006 presented borrowers with conflicting incentives. On the one hand, Figure 2 shows that rates on 30-year fixed mortgages were generally around 6% during 2004 through 2006, low by historical standards. Borrowers had an incentive to use fixed rate mortgages to lock-in these low rates. On the other hand, Figure 2 also shows that the gap between short- and long-term rates was relatively large in 2004. The larger this gap, the more a borrower benefits from an adjustable-rate mortgage, which tends to follow short-term rates. Also, the benefit of an adjustable rate mortgage is greater if the borrower intends to quickly sell the house or refinance the loan — which coincides with rapidly appreciating housing markets.

The use of mortgage products with introductory periods and adjustable interest rates arguably was a reasonable response to house price appreciation and interest rates in 2004. By 2005, however, short-term interest rates were rising faster than long-term interest rates. Yet, adjustable rates remained very popular. House price appreciation slowed significantly in 2006, yet introductory periods remained popular. The persistence of nontraditional terms could be evidence that some borrowers intended to sell or refinance quickly — one indicator of speculative behavior.

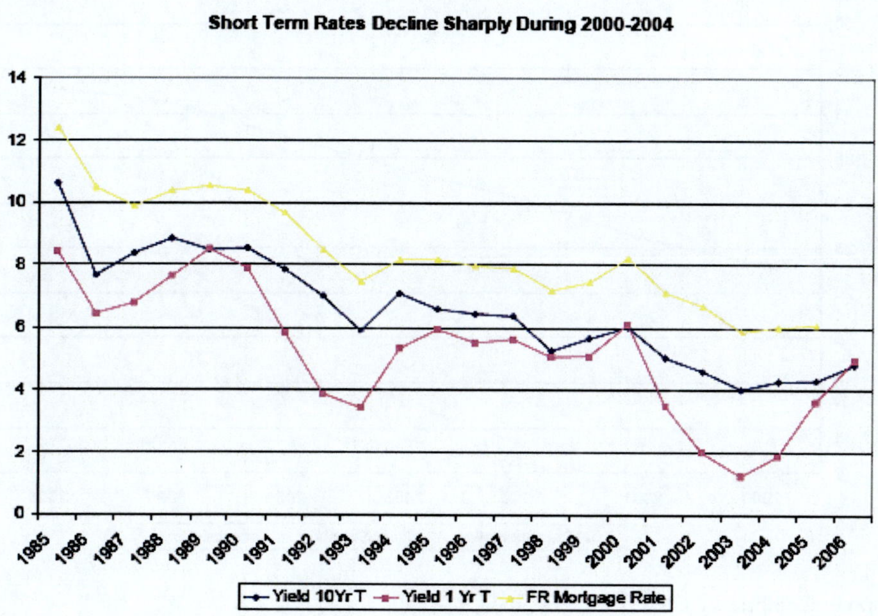

Source: Federal Reserve.

Figure 2. Falling Interest Rates Fueled Housing Markets.

Credit Quality of Resetting Loans Appears Weak

As the reset dates of billions of dollars of subprime mortgages near, analysts want to know the quality of the underwriting that was used when the loans were originated. For 2-28s and 3-27s, this requires information on the risk-characteristics of loans originated in prior years. Information from industry sources suggests that non-agency subprime loans became more risky as the housing boom progressed. For example, Figure 3 shows that the percent of subprime loans with low documentation doubled between 2000 and 2005.[5] Similarly, the percent of subprime loans that used silent seconds to avoid private mortgage insurance (PMI) increased from almost none in 2000 to 25% of the subprime market by 2006.[6] Figure 3 also shows the increased use of subprime loans with interest-only periods, which require higher resets even if interest rates do not rise.

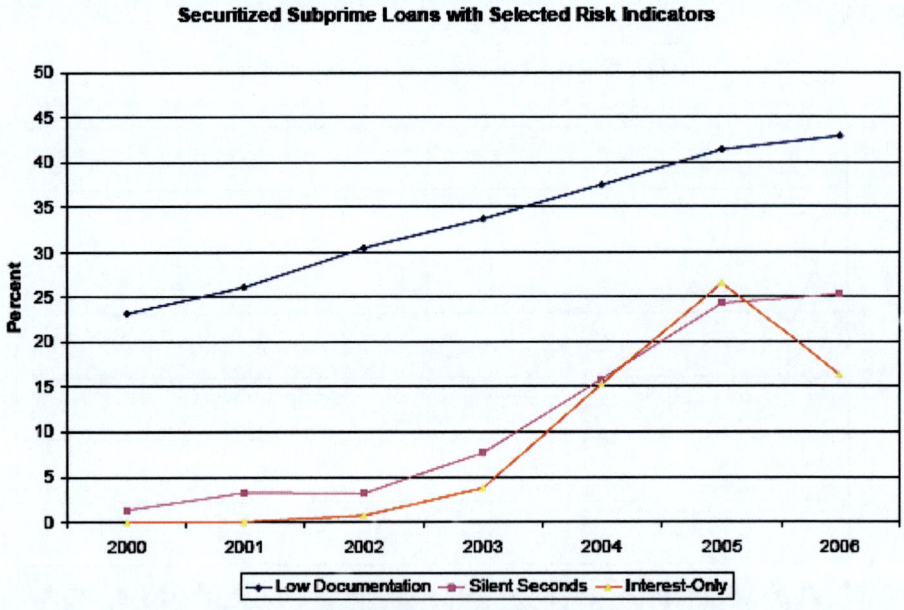

Source: Compile by CRS from UBS data.

Figure 3. Underwriting Standards Weakened.

In summary, falling interest rates had two important effects on alternative mortgage markets. First, lower mortgage rates initially helped bid up house prices as households qualified for larger loans, which increased appreciation rates.

Second, the incentive to use adjustable rate mortgages increased because short-term rates initially fell faster than long-term rates. House price appreciation and low interest rates, which many expected to continue, encouraged the use of mortgages that reset and have substantially higher future payments. Subsequent increases in interest rates and slowing house prices have resulted in some unsustainable resets and the forecast of more unsustainable resets. Understanding the choice of mortgages containing a reset requires an examination of the features of nontraditional mortgages.

FEATURES OF NONTRADITIONAL MORTGAGES

Discussions of alternative mortgages often focus on some combination of four differences from traditional mortgages. Borrowers increasingly chose one or more of the following features:

adjustable rates,
extremely low or zero down payment,
interest-only payments, and
negative amortization.

Adjustable Rates

There are many varieties of adjustable rate mortgages (ARMs). One of the simplest forms offers an initial low rate, called a teaser, at the beginning of the loan and then resets after an introductory period. The teaser rate may apply for one year or for as little as one month. The mortgage contract may specify a reset interest rate or may tie the rate to another interest rate by formula. The resulting interest rate may itself be fixed or variable. Teaser rates should be distinguished from fully adjustable rate mortgages. In principle, a 30-year fixed rate mortgage could have a one-month teaser rate without materially affecting the costs and benefits of the mortgage product.

Excluding teaser rates, variable rate mortgages tie the loan to the economy. The future mortgage rate on these loans typically depends on another future interest rate observed in financial markets. The rate might reset each month, each year, or only after several years. The home buyer's mortgage payment would drop if the interest rate dropped but would rise if the interest rate rose. Many adjustable rate mortgages provide for a cap on the amount a rate can rise in any period or over the life of the loan.

Adjustable rate mortgages can be tied to a variety of market interest rates. One common reference rate is the London Interbank Offered Rate (LIBOR). LIBOR rates are determined in the London market for unsecured bank loans. It is a rate that banks charge each other for short term loans (less than 12 months). Typical adjustable rate mortgages will specify a reset date at which time the mortgage rate will adjust to the LIBOR or similar rate plus a predetermined markup.

Extremely Low or Zero Down Payment

Saving enough funds to meet the traditional 20% down payment can be a significant barrier to otherwise credit-worthy potential home buyers. Furthermore, the required down payment grows with the appreciation rate. If home appreciation is growing faster than household income, then it will be difficult for first time home buyers to save sufficiently. Lending programs gradually reduced the required down payment options to 10%, 5%, and eventually 3% of the purchase price. There are mortgages that take this process to its logical conclusion and allow buyers to purchase with no money down. Some programs even roll in closing and other acquisition costs for greater-than-100% financing.

A related practice is using a second mortgage to finance the down payment. Sometimes called piggy back loans or silent seconds, the home buyer uses the second loan to borrow the funds for a 20% down payment. This down payment is enough to improve the interest rate and other terms of the first mortgage. However, the second mortgage carries a higher interest rate and other less desirable features because the first mortgage has prior claim on the collateral. Although the original first-mortgage lender may be aware of the piggy back loan (and may have helped arrange it), subsequent holders of the first mortgage may not be aware of the piggy back loan because lenders often sell the loans they originate to the secondary mortgage market.

Interest Only

An interest-only mortgage allows the home buyer to carry the loan balance for a period of time without having to pay back any principal. The current mortgage payment covers only the monthly interest due on the existing balance.

Eventually, the monthly payment must also cover the principal. If the duration of the mortgage is not extended, then the payments will have to amortize the remaining balance over a shorter period of time. Therefore, a homeowner choosing to pay only the interest for a few months increases the monthly payment for later months.

Negative Amortization

Unlike interest-only mortgages which leave the loan balance unchanged, a mortgage with negative amortization allows the borrower to increase the loan's principal by paying less than the current interest due. The remaining interest is added to the loan balance. Future payments are then recalculated based on the increased principal. The homeowner gets lower current payments but at the cost of greater debt and higher future payments.

These four features of alternative mortgages are not mutually exclusive. There are option mortgages which allow borrowers to choose each month to pay a fully amortizing amount, an interest-only amount, or a negatively amortizing amount. Interest-only mortgages that use an adjustable rate when the introductory period ends are also common. The increased use of these mortgages and innovative combination of features has drawn the attention of federal regulators.

Federal Agency Actions on Alternative Mortgages

Financial Regulatory Institution Guidance

Several federal banking agencies, including the Federal Reserve, the Office of Thrift Supervision (OTS), the National Credit Union Agency (NCUA), the Federal Deposit Insurance Corporation (FDIC), and the Office of the Comptroller of the Currency (OCC), oversee mortgage originations by financial institutions. These agencies are all part of the Federal Financial Institutions Examination Council (FFIEC), and issued a joint guidance statement (the 10/06 Guidance) for alternative mortgages on October 4, 2006.[7] This guidance applies to federally regulated financial institutions but not to many non-bank lenders in the subprime sector. In addition to inter-agency guidance, the Federal Reserve revised Regulation Z under the Truth in Lending Act (TILA) in July 2008. Regulation Z applies to all mortgage lenders.

October 2006 Inter-Agency Guidance

Issues and Comments

The FFIEC agencies are responsible for overseeing both the consumer protection mandates of the Truth in Lending Act (TILA) and the safety and soundness of their regulated institutions. The agencies recognized that alternative mortgages have existed for some time but were concerned that products with possible negative amortization were being offered to a wider spectrum of borrowers by greater numbers of lenders. The 10/06 Guidance addressed three areas of concern: underwriting standards, risk management, and consumer protection. The 10/06 Guidance specified that lenders must tighten underwriting standards to manage risk. Lenders must also provide clear information to consumers to ensure consumer protection, but the guidance explicitly rejected imposing the doctrine of suitability.[8]

The comment period drew a range of views on the proposal that became the 10/06 Guidance. Some depository institutions and industry groups argued against additional restrictions on alternative mortgages. They pointed out that alternatives to the traditional 30-year fixed rate mortgage have been successfully used for many years. Some argued that alternative mortgages contribute to market flexibility in a changing economy. Some also argued that lenders had the incentive and the capability to appropriately manage the risks.

Critics of alternative mortgages encouraged more stringent limitations. Some argued that an agency guidance would not be effective enough because it would not apply to lenders regulated at the state level. These critics argued for new federal legislation. Some consumer groups argued that alternative mortgages were too complex for unsophisticated borrowers to fully understand. Others argued that expanded use of nontraditional mortgages could encourage speculation in real estate and destabilize house prices.

Consumer Disclosure

The 10/06 Guidance addressed some of the commenters' consumer protection concerns. Lenders are to provide full disclosure in plain language. Lenders were already required to give consumers considering adjustable rate mortgages an information booklet published by the Federal Reserve.[9]

The 10/06 Guidance now requires that consumers considering other nontraditional mortgages be given similar information including examples of payment comparisons. As of August 2007, the the FFIEC has not issued a mandatory interest-only or negative-amortization counterpart to the adjustable rate booklet, although the Office of the Comptroller of the Currency has a model booklet.

The Government Accountability Office (GAO) also made recommendations for alternative mortgages. On disclosures, GAO found that "although federal banking regulators have taken a range of proactive steps to address AMP [alternative mortgage product] lending, current federal standards for disclosures do not require information on AMP specific risks."[10] GAO recommended that the Federal Reserve improve its regulations governing disclosures by requiring language that explains the specific risks and features of alternative mortgages.

Prudent Practices

In addition to consumer disclosure, the 10/06 Guidance addresses a number of lending practices that some commenters considered unsafe or unsound. The use of alternative mortgages by less affluent borrowers raised concerns that some home buyers would not be able to sustain payments if housing market conditions changed. The 10/06 Guidance specifically addresses collateral-dependent loans, risk layering, and third-party relationships.

The 10/06 Guidance stated that collateral dependent loans are an unsafe and unsound lending practice. Collateral-dependent loans refers to the practice of lenders to rely solely on the borrower's ability to sell or refinance the property to approve the loan. An example of this practice would be an interest-only loan to a person with no down payment that resets after three or five years. In the first few years of the loan, the borrower is expected to pay a high interest rate. When the loan resets, the buyer is expected to refinance the loan, by which time appreciation could have provided a down payment which would reduce the interest rate the buyer would be expected to pay.

The 10/06 Guidance requires loans to be underwritten for full risk layering. To understand risk layering, consider a mortgage with an optional negative amotization feature. This option is the equivalent of extending the borrower additional credit without additional underwriting. If the borrower chooses to pay less than current interest in the current month, then the remaining interest is added to the loan balance. For example, a borrower may be extended a $200,000 loan that could rise to a $250,000 balance if the borrower pays the minimum each period. The 10/06 Guidance specifies that lenders consider a borrower's ability to repay the maximum loan balance assuming the borrower pays only the minimum monthly payment each period. In the example, the lender would have to qualify the borrower for a $250,000 loan, not a $200,000 loan.

The 10/06 Guidance also addresses third-party relationships and risk management. Banks and financial institutions often do not originate or hold their loans. Mortgage brokers may market the loans to consumers. Once originated, the loans may be sold to investors in the secondary mortgage market. The guidance requires covered institutions to have strong systems and controls for establishing and maintaining third party relationships. While the industry worried that this would require institutions to oversee the marketing practices of third-parties, the agencies responded that an institution's risk management system should address the overall level of risk that third-party relationships create for the institution.

FEDERAL RESERVE REVISION OF REGULATION Z

Consumer Protection Hearings

The Federal Reserve administers the consumer protection laws that apply to all lenders, even non-bank lenders that are not subject to agency guidances. The Federal Reserve used the notice and comment rulemaking procedures to modify protections for consumers in mortgage transactions. After a series of hearings had been held on the Truth in Lending Act and the Home Owners Equity Protection Act, which the Federal Reserve implements through Regulation Z, the Federal Reserve revised rules.

The Board heard testimony focusing on four questions regarding its HOEPA authority: (1) should prepayment penalties be restricted to the introductory periods of resetting loans; (2) should escrow accounts for taxes and insurance be mandated for subprime loans (the practice is common in prime markets; (3) should limitations be put on stated income loans, also known as low-doc loans or even liar loans; and (4) should additional limits be placed on underwriting loans based on a borrower's ability to pay out of household income, rather than the value of the collateral?

Final Rule for Regulation Z

The Federal Reserve issued its final rule for Regulation Z on July 14, 2008. Some of the changes made by the Federal Reserve apply only to higher prices loans whereas others apply to all mortgage loans. In addition, the Federal Reserve adjusted its definition of higher priced loans to account for the effect of the gap between short-term and long-term interest rates, as well as lowering the threshold for designation as higher cost.

The Federal Reserve made several significant changes to the rules that apply to the origination of all mortgage loans secured by a principal dwelling. It bans creditors and mortgage brokers from coercing a real estate appraiser to misstate a home's value. It also bans pyramiding late fees and certain other mortgage servicing practices. In addition, lenders and servicers are required to credit borrowers' mortgage payments as of the date of receipt and provide a statement. Borrowers must receive a good faith estimate of the loan costs, including a schedule of payments, within three days after application for all mortgage loans. Consumers cannot be charged any fee until after they receive the early disclosures, except a reasonable fee for obtaining the consumer's credit history.

Some of the changes to Regulation Z apply only to higher priced mortgages. These include prohibiting a lender from making a loan without regard to borrowers' ability to repay the loan from income and assets other than the home's value (so-called collateral dependent lending). For higher price loans, the new rule requires creditors to verify the income and assets they rely upon to determine the borrower's ability to repay the loan. It places a ban on prepayment penalties if the monthly mortgage payment can change in the first four years. For other higher-priced loans, a prepayment penalty period cannot last for more than two years. The rule also requires creditors to establish escrow accounts for property taxes and homeowner's insurance for all first-lien mortgage loans.

FHA's Hope for Homeowners Program

Policymakers enacted the Hope for Homeowners Program in July 2008 (H.R. 3221 / P.L. 110-289). This program allows lenders and borrowers to voluntarily refinance troubled mortgages into an FHA-insured loan. To participate, borrowers must certify that their loan was unaffordable as of March 2008 and lenders must agree to write-down the principal of the loan to a more affordable level. The program allows for up to $300 billion in FHA-insured loans in which the borrower would be responsible for 90% of the new appraised value. The lenders would write-down the loan an additional 4.5% to cover the one time premium and the first annual premium of the FHA insurance. Therefore, the lender must agree to write down the loan to 85.5% of the current appraised value, and in some areas the current appraisal may be significantly below the original loan balance. The FHA loan limit was increased in high cost areas to as much as $625,000. The act also provided for more flexibility for some of FHA's underwriting criteria.[11]

Analysis of Nontraditional Mortgages

GAO estimates that interest-only and other alternative mortgages approached 30% of the mortgage market by 2005.[12] Payments on these mortgages will reset to higher levels in the next few years. Although such products were sometimes used in the past by sophisticated borrowers as cash management tools, the recent housing boom saw alternative mortgages offered as affordability products to less sophisticated borrowers. Alternative mortgages were used by less wealthy borrowers in areas of high expected appreciation. The concentration of mortgage resets in time and in location can cause concerns for individual borrowers, for local real estate markets, and for financial institutions.

Payment Resets, Affordability Products, and Planned Refinances

The expanded use of alternative mortgages during the housing boom has created a wave of mortgage resets due in the next few years as the introductory periods expire. Not only do adjustable rate mortgages change their payments as interest rates change, but interest-only mortgages increase their payments when the full amortization period begins. Even if interest rates do not increase much further, the increase in monthly payments is substantial for many borrowers.

Consider a $200,000 interest-only loan originated at a time when the prevailing mortgage rate is 6.5%. The interest-only period lasts four years then the loan amortizes over the final 26 years at the 6.5 percent rate. The monthly payments during the interest-only period will be $1,083. The monthly payments increase to $1,328 after four years. Even though the borrower will not be affected if interest rates rise above 6.5 percent, monthly payments will still rise $245 per month. Table 1 compares this hypothetical interest-only loan to a similar fully amortizing fixed rate mortgage. Although the early payments of the interest-only mortgage are lower than the traditional mortgage, the later payments are higher.

Table 1. Payment Reset for Interest-Only Mortgages

Interest Only (I/O) Feature and Payment Increases for $200,000 Loan at 6.5% Interest				
	Initial Payments	Reset Payments	Change	Percentage Increase
Traditional 30 Year Fixed	$1,264	$1,264	$0	0%
I/O, Reset Year 5	$1,083	$1,328	$245	23%

Source: Table prepared by the Congressional Research Service (CRS).

Unlike interest-only mortgages, adjustable rate mortgages could have declining payments as well as rising payments. Adjustable rate mortgages were very common in the 1980s when interest rates were high and many people expected mortgage rates to fall. The concern with more-recent adjustable rate mortgages is that their original rate was near historic lows so it is probable that the prevailing interest rate will be higher when they reset.[13] (Interest rate risk will be discussed in greater detail below.) Table 2 presents sample payment resets after three years for a $200,000 mortgage if interest rates rise or fall by a few percentage points. If the interest rate was originally 6%, then the monthly mortgage payment is $1199. If interest rates rise to 8%, then the monthly mortgage payment rises to $1449. On the other hand, if interest rates fall to 4%, then the monthly payment would drop to $971.

Table 2. Payment Reset for Adjustable Rates Mortgages

Interest Rates and Monthly Payments Fully Amortizing $200,000 Loan, 30 Years Rate Resets After 3 Years		
	Interest Rate	Monthly Payment
	4%	$971
	5%	$1,082
Base Rate	6%	$1199
	7%	$1322
	8%	$1449
	9%	$1582
	10%	$1718

Sophisticated borrowers have used alternative mortgages to manage their cash flow for a long time. Consider a person who can qualify for any type of loan and has plenty of savings for contingencies. If the person must move frequently for work, then the person might not care much about the size of later payments because the loan will not extend that long. If a couple starts in a one-bedroom condominium but expects to move when they have children, then they might not want a traditional mortgage. If the person has other interest-rate-sensitive investments, then the person might use the mortgage as a hedge. For example, the holder of adjustable rate bonds would lose if interest rates fell but could offset part of that loss through an adjustable rate mortgage.

Alternative mortgages were marketed as affordability products to lower income and less sophisticated borrowers during the housing boom. This raises concerns that some home buyers applied for more debt than they could qualify for using traditional underwriting standards. Lenders may have qualified them for the greater debt through these alternative products. In some cases, underwriting standards became more lax even using traditional qualifying ratios because the process was based on the early years of an alternative mortgage product's payments. As a result, underwriters are now qualifying people based on the maximum payment, called the fully indexed rate.

Consider again the $200,000 loan at 6.5% presented in Table 1. Traditionally, lenders presumed that there was a cap on the percentage of household income borrowers could devote to housing costs. If that cap was 28%, and the traditional 30- year fixed rate mortgage had monthly payments of $1,264, then a borrower would need an income of $54,177 to qualify for the traditional loan. A borrower with a lower income could not qualify for that loan and presumably could not buy the house.

The interest-only loan presents an interesting qualifying issue. If households can devote 28% of income to housing costs, then an income of $46,428 qualifies for the early years of the loan. However, an income of $56,950 would be required for the later years of the interest-only loan. Table 3 compares the income required to support the monthly payment assuming that households can devote 28% to housing costs. A borrower with only $46,428 might be tempted to take out a $200,000 loan using the interest-only product and then refinance the house when the payment reset.

Table 3. Payment Driven Loan Qualification

$200,000 Loan Using 28% Qualifying Ratio		
Loan Type	Payment	Qualifying Income
I/O Years 1-5	$1,083	$46,428
FRM 30 Years	$1,264	$54,177
I/O Years 6-30	$1,328	$56,950

Source: Table prepared by the Congressional Research Service (CRS).

A cash-constrained borrower's ability to successfully execute the planned refinancing would depend on the housing market. The borrower is relying on the expected appreciation of the house itself to help pay for the house. This is an example of a collateral-dependent loan which the 10/06 Guidance designates unsafe and unsound. It is not known how many of the loans due to reset in the next two years are collateral-dependent loans. The performance of these loans will depend on the housing market.

Reasons for the Resets: Booming House Prices and the Attraction of Alternative Mortgages

U.S. house prices appreciated rapidly in many regions during 2001 through 2005. Nationally, the Office of Federal Housing Enterprise Oversight (OFHEO) house price index (HPI) rose 51% over the five-year period. Table 4 compares appreciation during the recent boom to appreciation in other five-year periods. The recent housing boom saw the fastest appreciation since 1980. The boom stands out even more when it is adjusted for inflation. Real house prices rose 34% between 2000 and 2005.

Table 4. U.S. House Price Appreciation, 1980-2005

Nominal and Real Change in OFHEO House Price Index (HPI) 5-Year Increments					
	1980-85	1985-90	1990-95	1995-00	2000-05
Nominal HPI	25%	37%	8%	26%	51%
Real HPI	-8%	14%	-9%	12%	34%

Source: Office of Federal Housing Enterprise Oversight (OFHEO).

The distinction between nominal and real house prices is important. Mortgage contracts are almost always specified in nominal terms. This means that a fall in the real price might not cause a borrower to be upside down on the mortgage if inflation is high enough to counteract the real price decline. This scenario occurred in the early 1980s and the early 1990s. On the other hand, analysts considering the return to housing as an investment often focus on real prices.[14] Although real prices can be important for long term trends in the composition of household savings, nominal prices are more important for determining the stress on borrowers as their payment reset date nears.

Prices rose even more rapidly in some markets. Table 5 compares the annual appreciation rate of some U.S. cities during 2000 through 2006. The extremely rapid rise in certain markets led to concerns that the 1990s stock bubble had been replaced with a housing bubble.[15] For example, Las Vegas house prices rose 34.9% in a single year, 2004. Orlando's house prices rose 32.7% in 2005. Seven of the cities listed in Table 5 experienced five consecutive years of appreciation rates exceeding 10% per year. Then in 2006, the housing market slowed dramatically, as shown by the significant decline in the appreciation rate in each of the 31 cities listed in Table 5.

Table 5. Annual House Price Appreciation, 2000-2006, by Metro Area

	2000	2001	2002	2003	2004	2005	2006	AVG 00-05
US National	8.1%	6.5%	7.1%	8.2%	13.0%	12.9%	2.1%	9.3%
West Palm Beach	8.7	11.2	13.6	17.0	27.1	28.7	0.2	17.7
Los Angeles	8.9	10.5	14.3	19.3	27.0	23.6	4.4	17.3
Miami	9.1	13.0	14.1	15.2	22.7	28.7	8.4	17.1
Washington	11.7	11.3	10.9	14.0	24.2	22.3	2.7	15.7
San Diego	13.4	11.9	16.6	17.7	25.9	8.7	-0.1	15.7
Las Vegas	6.6	5.9	5.9	18.3	34.9	16.6	1.3	14.7
Orlando	8.7	6.9	7.9	9.1	20.4	32.7	5.5	14.3
Phoenix	6.5	5.4	4.9	6.9	22.2	37.0	3.8	13.8
New York	10.8	10.9	11.3	11.8	16.3	16.6	1.9	13.0
San Francisco	19.2	2.9	6.6	6.3	18.9	15.1	1.2	11.5
Philadelphia	7.1	8.5	9.6	11.3	15.9	14.2	3.0	11.1
Boston	13.6	12.5	12.2	10.3	11.6	5.9	-1.2	11.0
Richmond	5.5	5.3	6.5	8.2	13.6	17.8	4.3	9.5
Minneapolis	11.0	10.2	8.3	8.7	9.5	6.7	0.3	9.1
Portland	5.0	4.0	4.0	6.0	12.7	12.6	7.5	8.9
Chicago	6.7	7.4	6.3	7.7	11.1	10.8	2.9	8.3
New Orleans	5.9	3.8	6.0	6.4	8.3	14.9	5.4	7.6
St. Louis	6.4	6.3	5.2	6.6	8.6	7.6	1.9	6.8
Birmingham	6.4	3.2	4.7	4.7	6.0	8.9	2.3	5.6
Pittsburgh	7.4	4.8	4.5	5.0	5.3	5.6	0.3	5.4
Denver	12.2	6.2	3.3	2.7	3.9	3.5	1.0	5.3
Kansas City	6.5	5.6	4.6	4.0	5.7	5.5	0.5	5.3
Atlanta	8.4	5.0	4.4	3.6	4.9	5.1	1.6	5.2
Buffalo	6.0	3.8	4.2	5.0	6.5	5.4	2.4	5.1
Nashville	5.2	2.8	2.6	3.7	6.2	9.2	4.8	5.0
Houston	7.1	4.0	4.6	3.4	4.7	5.8	2.8	4.9
Cincinnati	5.7	3.8	3.5	3.4	5.2	4.2	0.9	4.3
Detroit	7.4	5.4	3.6	3.4	3.4	1.8	-3.0	4.2
Dallas	7.1	4.1	3.7	2.1	3.1	4.1	1.9	4.0
Charlotte	5.9	2.4	2.9	2.2	4.2	6.1	4.4	3.9
Cleveland	5.6	3.3	3.6	3.8	4.0	2.6	-0.8	3.8

Source: OFHEO HPI, calculated 1_{st} Quarter to 1_{st} Quarter.

Markets with rapid appreciation reduce the ability of first-time buyers to save for down payments. A 20% down payment on a $200,000 house is $40,000. If prices rise 10%, then the 20% down payment rises to $44,000. The down payment becomes a moving target. In areas with rapid home price appreciation, the required down payment may be growing faster than household income. Potential first time buyers may fear being permanently priced out of the market if they do not enter the market as soon as possible.

While rapid home price appreciation may outstrip the savings of renters, an owner's home price appreciation actually increases household savings. Home equity is a form of savings for home owners. Including the growth in home equity, savings rise faster if the household is an owner in a rapidly appreciating market but the household can't become an owner until it has accumulated sufficient savings for a down payment. A mortgage with a low down payment that is designed to be refinanced after a few years could allow the prospective first-time home buyer to get in to the market and take advantage of the house's growing equity.

Rapid appreciation can reduce the time needed for credit enhancement. Lenders typically require some form of credit enhancement if the value of the loan is more than 80% of the value of the property. This loan-to-value ratio (LTV) of 0.8 corresponds with the traditional 20% down payment. One way that buyers with less than 20% down enhanced their credit was through private mortgage insurance (PMI). However, the PMI monthly premium counted towards the funds that underwriters assumed households could devote to housing costs. The more quickly that a household can lower LTV and eliminate the need for PMI, the greater the percentage of the household's total monthly payment can be devoted to paying off the loan. In rapidly appreciating markets, the effect of growing equity on potential savings and on the need for PMI made alternative mortgages with planned refinances a potential affordability product. If first time buyers could just get into the rising market, then the growing equity would provide sufficient savings to lower LTV and eliminate the need for PMI by the time they had to refinance. Similar logic applies if buyers replace PMI with a piggy back loan at a higher interest rate because the need for the second loan at a higher rate is eliminated when equity rises.

Table 6 presents the growth of equity and reduction in LTV for a $200,000 interest-only loan for various appreciation rates. If appreciation rises 10%, then by the beginning of year three the equity increases to $42,000 and the LTV falls to 0.79. In this case, the buyer who put zero down and paid only interest would be able to refinance into a loan without credit enhancement because the drop in LTV is the equivalent of the 20% down payment. The time required to reduce LTV enough to eliminate credit enhancement decreases as the appreciation rate rises.

The preceding discussion showed two ways that zero down payment and interest-only mortgages could have been used as affordability products. First, if qualification is payment driven, then lower-income borrowers could be qualified based on the payments required during the introductory period of interest-only mortgages

Table 6. Appreciation, Home Equity, and Loan to Value (LTV)

Appreciation Contribution to Home Equity $200,000 House, Zero Down, I/O Loan Reset Year Appreciation Rate (Annual Percent)										
Beginning Year	0% Equity	LTV	5% Equity	LTV	10% Equity	LTV	15% Equity	LT V	20% Equity	LTV
1	0	1	$0	1.00	$0	1.00	$0	1.00	$0	1.00
2	0	1	10,000	0.95	20,000	0.90	30,000	0.85	40,000	0.80
3	0	1	20,000	0.90	42,000	0.79	64,500	0.68	88,000	0.56
4	0	1	31,525	0.84	66,200	0.67	104,175	0.48	145,600	0.27
5	0	1	43,101	0.78	92,820	0.54	149,801	0.25	214,720	-0.07

Source: CRS Calculations.

. Table 3 showed that a household with $46,428 income could qualify for the early payments of a $200,000 loan at 6.5% interest, even though that loan would have traditionally required an income of $54,177 to qualify. Second, price appreciation during the introductory period could lower LTV, eliminate the need for credit enhancement, and allow the household to devote more funds to the house payment. Table 6 showed that 10% annual appreciation can eliminate the need for PMI by the beginning of the third year of payments.

Problems arose when the housing market weakened further. Some of these borrowers are not able to refinance prior to their payment reset dates because their houses failed to appreciate at the expected rate.

Negative Appreciation: Consequences for Resets

Borrowers using alternative mortgages to take advantage of appreciation are exposed to the risk that house prices will fail to appreciate or even decline in price. Recall that Table 5 showed that the rate of appreciation slowed across the country in 2006. In some formerly hot markets, prices declined in 2006 and the first half of 2007. As payment reset dates approach, many borrowers who used alternative mortgages as affordability products will wish to refinance. Their ability to refinance is obstructed, in many cases, by the failure to achieve home equity through price appreciation.

Local factors usually play a dominant role in determining regional house prices. Because of the role the job market plays in household income, analysts assume the local unemployment rate is important even in the absence of other information. For example, David Lereah, chief economist for the National Association of Realtors, emphasized the labor market in a presentation to residents of Charleston, SC. "Your unemployment situation is very positive ... I really don't know the local industries in Charleston other than tourism, but whatever it is, it's doing a good job."[16] Although Lereah went on to discuss migration patterns and other factors, the stress on labor markets is unmistakable.

Because local economies often play such a crucial role in house prices, one might think that the price risks embodied in low down payment mortgages is only a problem if an area's unemployment rises. While it is true that an increase in local unemployment can help drive down house prices, it is important to note that prices can fall even if the local labor market is healthy. The next sections show how different metro areas can have divergent price trends but that the recent house price slowdown is widespread and independent of local unemployment.

House prices in different metro areas do not always follow the national trend or move in the same direction. Recall again the wide range of appreciation rates for the cities presented in Table 5. San Diego's houses appreciated over 15% per year during 2000-2005, but Denver and Buffalo were closer to 5% per year. Figure 4 tracks house prices for San Diego, Buffalo, and Denver from 1980 to 2005. They do not follow the national average nor do they follow similar patterns. Denver's prices rose more quickly in the early 1980s, when San Diego and Buffalo stagnated. San Diego boomed in the late 1980s but then fell in the 1990s. Buffalo's prices followed a more stable trajectory. Differences in the local economies of the three cities contributed to the divergent paths of home prices.

Many of the biggest house price slowdowns in 2006 cannot be attributed to shocks to local job markets. For example, Boston's appreciation rate dropped during 2004-2006 even though the Massachusetts labor market remained stable. Boston's appreciation rate fell from 11.6% in 2004, to 5.9% in 2005, and finally fell 1.2% in the first three quarters of 2006. Yet the Massachusetts unemployment rate remained close to 5% in all three years.[17] Despite a relatively stable labor market, Boston's house prices stopped appreciating.

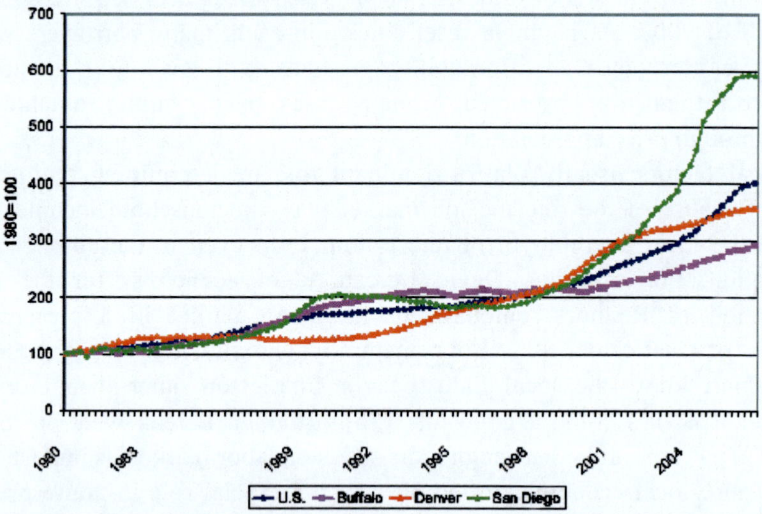

Source: OFHEO House Price Index.

Figure 4. Comparison of Appreciation for 3 Cities, 1980-2005.

Table 7. Local Unemployment and Slowing Appreciation

Local Unemployment and Slowing Appreciation				
Market	Unemployment		Appreciation	
	10/05	10/06	2005	2006
Phoenix	4.2%	3.4%	37.0%	3.8%
San Diego	4.2	3.6	8.7	-0.1
Los Angeles	4.5	3.9	23.6	4.4
New York	5.8	4.1	16.6	1.9
Miami	3.7	3.5	28.7	8.4
Washington	3.0	2.9	22.3	2.7
Las Vegas	3.7	4.0	16.6	1.3
Orlando	3.1	2.8	32.7	5.5

Source: OFHEO and BLS.

The slowdowns in house price appreciation were widespread and occurred in areas with healthy job markets. Table 7 compares local unemployment rate changes to the slowdown in appreciation for several of the formerly hot housing markets. Notice that the local unemployment rates were relatively unchanged in October 2006 compared to October 2005. Yet the rate of home price appreciation fell precipitously in each market. Table 7 shows that the rate of appreciation experienced by home buyers while they are choosing their mortgage can decline drastically even if the local economy remains healthy.

Zero or negative appreciation in an otherwise healthy economy is a problem for borrowers who made very low down payments. If they used a piggy back loan to avoid PMI or used an interest-only loan and planned to refinance when they reached an LTV of 0.8, then they may have become upside-down on the mortgage. Borrowers with little savings are finding it difficult to refinance or sell a house before the reset date because their LTV has not improved (i.e., declined). Table 8 shows how declines in house prices affect the LTV of zero-down borrowers for a $200,000 interest-only loan.

If house prices depreciate 3% per year for two years, then the zero-down, interest-only borrower presented in Table 8 will owe $11,820 more than the house is worth. Recall that one reason a borrower might have been attracted to the interestonly loan was because the borrower did not have the savings for a down payment. When the introductory period ends and the reset date arrives, the borrower's payments will rise.

Table 8. Negative Appreciation, Equity, and Loan to Value (LTV)

Negative Appreciation and Increasing Debt Burdens $200,000 House, Zero Down, I/O Loan Reset Year 5										
	0%		-1%		-2%		-3%		-4%	
Begin Year	Equity	LTV	Equity	LTV	Equity	LTV	Equity	LTV	Equity	LTV
1	$0	1.00	$0	1.00	$0	1.00	$0	1.00	$0	1.00
2	$0	1.00	$-2,000	1.01	$-4,000	1.02	$-6,000	1.03	$-8,000	1.04
3	$0	1.00	$-3,980	1.02	$-7,920	1.04	$-11,820	1.06	$-15,680	1.08
4	$0	1.00	$-5,940	1.03	$-11,762	1.06	$-17,465	1.09	$-23,053	1.12
5	$0	1.00	$-7,881	1.04	$-15,526	1.08	$-22,941	1.11	$-30,131	1.15

Source: CRS Calculations.

In this hypothetical example of a $200,000 interest-only loan in a period of 6.5% interest rates, Table 1 shows that the reset payment would rise $245 per month after four years. The borrower must either find an additional $245 per month to maintain the current mortgage or $11,820 to cover the reduction in equity and try to refinance even if interest rates do not rise.

Interest Rate Risk

Although the risk of slowing house price appreciation is already a reality, interest rates are still relatively low. Problems could become more severe for consumers that used adjustable rates if mortgage rates rise despite Federal Reserve attempts to lower short term rates. A common form of alternative mortgage employs adjustable interest rates. Adjustable rate mortgages shift the risk of rising interest rates from the lenders to the borrowers. Table 2 showed how a rise in interest rates could increase the payment on an adjustable rate mortgage. However, adjustable rate mortgages allow borrowers to benefit when interest rates fall. The availability and popularity of adjustable rate mortgages have changed with changing macroeconomic conditions.

When lenders held most of their loans in their own portfolio, fixed rate mortgages imposed significant costs when interest rates rose. The lenders' own costs of funds depended on the short-term interest rates prevalent as time progressed.[18] However, the lenders' income from their mortgages depended on the interest rates prevalent at the time the mortgages were originated. This is called borrowing short and lending long. Rising interest rates increase the lenders' cost of funds but the lenders' incomes do not rise. In response to strains on the banking sector as interest rates rose in the late 1970s and early 1980s, Congress encouraged wider use of adjustable rate mortgages.[19]

Mortgage rates are affected by conditions in the macroeconomy. Although the Federal Reserve does not directly set long term interest rates such as mortgage rates, Federal Reserve policy can determine short term interest rates and influence inflation. The mortgage rate incorporates expectations of future inflation because mortgages are repaid over long periods. Figure 5 compares inflation, mortgage rates, and the Federal Reserve discount rate since 1972. The three are related but notice that the steep rise in the discount rate after 2003 has resulted in only a minor rise in mortgage rates during the same period.

The 1980s exemplify an environment conducive to adjustable rate mortgages. Mortgage rates began to decline as the fear of inflation subsided. Expecting mortgage rates to fall, more people turned to adjustable rates. For example, 61% of the conventional mortgages originated in 1984 were adjustable.[20] Mortgage rates then declined from over 13% in 1984 to under 8% by 1993. Once mortgage rates stabilized, the popularity of adjustable rate mortgages declined. For example, only 12% of mortgages originated in 2001 were adjustable rates. This relatively longstanding response of borrowers to changing macroeconomic conditions distinguishes adjustable rate mortgages from the use of interest-only mortgages as affordability products described earlier.

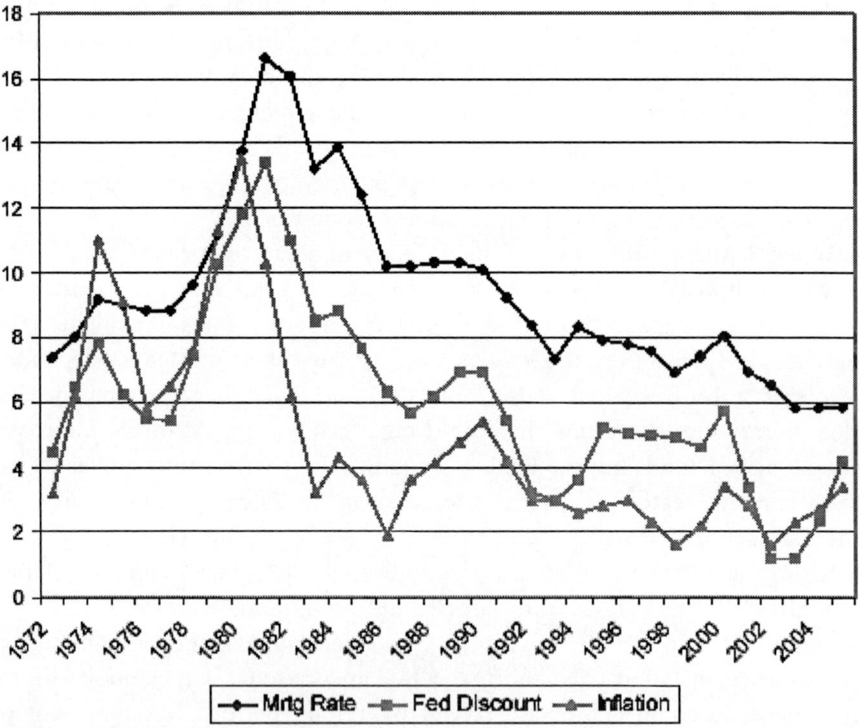

Source: Federal Reserve.

Figure 5. Mortgage Rate, Discount Rate, and Inflation, 1980-2005.

The pattern of adjustable rate mortgages during the recent boom suggests that borrowers accepted interest rate risk at a time when interest rates were at historic lows. Figure 5 showed that the mortgage rates prevailing in 2003-2005 represented 30-year lows. Consumers hedging against interest rate changes would be expected to lock in the historic low rates by borrowing at fixed rates. Yet the share of adjustable rates rose from 12% in 2001 to 34% in 2004, perhaps to take advantage of the large gap between short and long term interest rates. Although still well below the 61% share in 1984, the rising number of ARMs during a period of exceptionally low interest rates means that consumers shouldered additional interest rate risk as the boom progressed. There is evidence that this interest rate risk is concentrated in the formerly hot markets.

Geographic Correlation of Falling-House-Price Risk and Interest Rate Risk

Which regions are most vulnerable if a shortage of liquidity raises mortgage rates? Concentrated risk is important for cities as well as for financial institutions.

The presence of distressed neighbors affects the price that other sellers can get for their houses. If an area becomes concentrated with borrowers who are unprepared for payment shock and at the same time become upside down on their loans, then downward pressure can be put on housing prices. If this happens, then more homeowners will become upside down on their loans, reinforcing the problem. Exposure to the risk of rising interest rates is geographically concentrated in the areas that may be exposed to the risk of falling house prices.

The Federal Home Finance Board (FHFB) conducts a survey of the use of adjustable rate mortgages. The sample used for the survey excludes many important categories of nontraditional mortgages such as negatively amortizing loans. However, the survey can give some indication of the geographical concentration of some types of alternative mortgages and the exposure of some areas to the risk that inflation and interest rates will increase.

Table 9 uses FHFB data to show the use of adjustable rate mortgages and the recent slowdown in appreciation for 12 metropolitan areas from different parts of the country. The rates reported in Table 9 are unweighted averages of the five most recent quarters in the FHFB survey.[21] An area is more immediately exposed to rising interest rates if a higher percentage of its loans will reset interest rates in the near future. By this measure, Dallas and Houston are probably less exposed to the risk that interest rates might rise in the near future while California cities appear more exposed to interest rate risk.

In addition to a rise in interest rates for adjustable rate mortgages, regions could suffer if their lenders and home buyers used low down payments and overestimated the rate at which their houses would appreciate. Prior to the issuance of the 10/06 Guidance, some borrowers may have been using expected appreciation to get into larger houses than they could have otherwise afforded. Table 9 shows the decline in the rate of appreciation from 2005 to the first three quarters of 2006. To the extent that some borrowers counted on the rate of appreciation prevailing at the time they originated their loan to continue, a sudden deceleration in the rate of growth of prices will delay the time that they can achieve an LTV of 0.8 and get better terms when they attempt to refinance. Miami, California, and New York had comparatively large drops in appreciation and could have home buyers who made large mistakes when projecting appreciation rates.

Even though the appreciation rate might still be comparatively rapid, an unexpected drop in appreciation could still foil the plans of a low down payment buyer. For example, Miami's 2006 appreciation rate is still relatively high at 8%. However, if a zero-down Miami buyer in 2005 planned on appreciation of 20% per year and chose a mortgage that reset after one year, the 8% appreciation rate would not achieve the LTV of 0.8 to allow an improved refinance. The buyer wouldn't be upside down but would still pay more than expected costs because the loan might have to be refinanced more than once. Fees are paid each time a loan is refinanced.

Table 9 does not purport to measure the probability that a particular housing market will suffer severe stress. Instead, it is a very simple indication of a region's exposure to interest rate and falling-house-price risk. Industry analysts use more sophisticated methods to predict the probability that housing prices might fall in a particular market. The United States Market Risk index (USMR) is one such measure.[22]

The USMR index takes into account the local job market, recent price acceleration, and the affordability index. Weak job markets and low affordability tend to increase the risk of falling house prices. Stable recent appreciation tends to reduce the risk of falling house prices. Table 10 presents the market risk index for selected cities. A value of 100 implies a 10% chance that house prices in the area will fall within two years.

Table 9. Adjustable Rate Mortgages and Price Slowdowns

Loan Resets and Price Slowdown by Metro				
	Share of Adjustable Rates '06	Appreciation Rate		Falling Appreciation'05-'06
		'05	'06	
Atlanta	31%	5%	2%	
Boston	29%	6%	-1%	
Chicago	40%	11%	3%	
Dallas-Ft. Worth	11%	4%	2%	
Denver	36%	4%	1%	
Houston	9%	6%	3%	
Kansas City	16%	5%	1%	
Los Angeles	57%	24%	4%	
Miami	36%	29%	8%	
New York	30%	17%	2%	
San Diego	62%	9%	0%	
San Francisco	65%	15%	1%	

Source: FHFB and OFHEO.

Table 10 shows that areas with lower risk of falling house prices as measured by the PMI Group's USMR index tend to have fewer adjustable rate mortgages. The markets with a high percentage of adjustable rate mortgages are correlated with higher risk of falling house prices. Statistical analysis shows that the relationship of the risk of rising interest rates and the risk of falling house prices is positive.[23] There is a geographic concentration of mortgages vulnerable to rising interest rates and risks to any borrowers who made low down payments.

Washington, DC, and Chicago are notable exceptions. Chicago has a relatively high level of interest rate risk as measured by the share of adjustable rate loans but a low level of falling-house-price risk as measured by the USMR. Washington has a high risk of falling house prices but less interest rate risk.

A correlation of ARM share and the risk index does not imply causation. Nor is this a test of a formal model of the determination of regional ARM shares. Table 10 merely shows that the interest rate risk inherent in adjustable rate mortgages is correlated with the risk of falling house prices identified by PMI's market risk index. The regions using ARMs tend to be the regions most susceptible to changes in macroeconomic conditions such as interest rate changes.

Table 10. Adjustable Rate Mortgages and the Market Risk Index

Metropolitan Area	Share of Adjustable Rates 06	PMI Risk Index
San Francisco	65%	587
San Diego	62%	603
Los Angeles	57%	590
Las Vegas	51%	540
Sacramento	48%	601
Phoenix	41%	353
Chicago	40%	147
Seattle	39%	153
Miami	39%	471
Denver	36%	187
Orlando	34%	313
Tampa	34%	404
Portland	32%	158
Atlanta	31%	201
Milwaukee	31%	140
New York	30%	543
Boston	30%	596
Virginia Beach	29%	413
Minneapolis	27%	393
Detroit	25%	379
Columbus	24%	74
Washington	22%	540
St. Louis	21%	133
Indianapolis	19%	63
San Antonio	17%	78
Kansas City	16%	109
Philadelphia	13%	179
Dallas	11%	89
Cincinnati	9%	72
Houston	9%	88
Pittsburgh	6%	61
Cleveland	3%	74

Source: FHFB and PMI Group.

Recent Price Declines

The reversal in housing markets has been more severe than some regulators expected. In late 2006, OFHEO Chief Economist Patrick Lawler, for example, said "house prices continued to rise through the third quarter in most of the country, but generally at only low or moderate rates. The transition from sizzling markets to normal or weak markets has accelerated, and recent drops in interest rates have failed to stem precipitous price changes."[24] Although regulators may have been comforted by a study by the FDIC that reinforced the view that a slowdown in housing does not have to result in collapsing local markets, the result in 2008 has been falling house prices across the nation. Of 46 instances of housing booms in U.S. cities since 1978, 21 experienced a subsequent housing bust. In other words, more than half of the observations of housing booms were not followed by housing busts.[25] The housing busts that did occur were often associated with declines in the local area's predominant industries. In the present circumstances, however, housing markets declined even in areas with relatively healthy economies.

Conclusion

Mortgages with adjustable rates and interest-only options have been more widely used in recent years. Once only used by the financially sophisticated, products with significant payment adjustments have been marketed to low-income borrowers as affordable products. The performance of these products among lowerincome borrowers in the current stressed environment has been problematic.

The Federal Reserve has issued changes to Regulation Z that may provide improved disclosures for all mortgages, including those with alternative features. In addition, other bank regulatory agencies have issued guidance covering alternative mortgages, but these guidances do not apply to many non-bank lenders in the subprime market. Lenders must disclose adequate information to consumers in plain English. Lenders must take steps to manage the risks of alternative mortgages. These steps include assessing borrowers' capacity to pay the entire potential balance of negative amortization loans and establishing risk management procedures for third party loan partners. Lenders may not rely solely on the ability to sell the property to qualify borrowers for a loan.

By choosing interest-only products, some consumers face the risk of falling house prices as their reset period approaches. Their prospects do not appear good. By choosing adjustable rate mortgages, some consumers have shifted interest rate risk from lenders to themselves. The geographical distribution of alternative mortgages suggests that falling-house-price risk and interest rate risk are concentrated in the same regions. It remains to be seen if interest rates will remain low, but it is clear that some consumers did not adequately prepare for slowing appreciation. Rising numbers of bankruptcies among lenders suggests that many financial institutions also failed to adequately assess relevant risks.

REFERENCES

[1] "Facing the Fallout from Foreclosures," *Community Banker*, November 2006. p. 40.
[2] "Falling Prices Trap New Home Buyers," *Orange County Register*, December 13, 2006.
[3] When a borrower owes more than the collateral is worth, the borrower is said to be upside down.
[4] Subprime borrowers typically have significantly lower credit scores or other indicators of high risk while Alt-A borrowers have better credit but may have some other defect, such as reduced income documentation.
[5] "The U.S. Subprime Market: An Industry in Turmoil," Thomas Zimmerman, UBS, [http://www.prmia.org/chapter_pages/data/files/1471_2576_zimmerman%20presentation _presentation.pdf].
[6] A silent second is a second loan. It is often used as a substitute for a downpayment so that the first loan receives a lower interest rate. These loans are also sometimes used so that the first loan will be below the conforming loan limit and eligible for purchase by Fannie Mae and Freddie Mac, but then probably would not be found in this non-agency database.
[7] "Interagency Guidance on Nontraditional Mortgage Product Risks," *Federal Register*, vol. 71, October 4, 2006, p. 58613.
[8] The doctrine of suitability would impose a duty on lenders to ensure that a chosen mortgage product was suitable to the borrower's financial circumstances and goals.
[9] The Federal Reserve publishes the Consumer Handbook for Adjustable Rate Mortgages (CHARM Booklets). Regulation Z requires that consumers be given CHARM booklets in the shopping phase if they ask for, or are offered, adjustable rate mortgages.
[10] U.S. Government Accountability Office, Alternative Mortgage Products: Impact on Defaults Remains Unclear, But Disclosure of Risks to Borrowers Could be Improved, GAO- 06-11 12T, September 20, 2006. p. 2.
[11] For a discussion of FHA and related reform proposals, see CRS Report RS20530, *FHA Loan Insurance Program: An Overview*, by Bruce E.

Foote and Meredith Peterson, and CRS Report RS22662, *H.R. 1852 and Revisiting the FHA Premium Pricing Structure: Proposed Legislation in the 110th Congress*, by Darryl E. Getter.

[12] Alternative Mortgage Products, September 20, 2006.

[13] Some adjustable rates are tied to short-term interest rates while traditional mortgages are long term. Some sophisticated borrowers choose adjustable or fixed rate mortgages based on the difference between short- and long-term rates, called the yield curve. For these borrowers, the steepness of the yield curve, not the relation of current mortgage rates to their long-term trend, would be the important consideration.

[14] Robert Schiller's critique of the housing market uses real prices and attempts to adjust for changes in housing quality. See "Be Warned: Mr. Bubble is Worried Again," New York Times, August 21, 2005.

[15] When asked about a national housing bubble, former Federal Reserve Chairman Alan Greenspan replied that there was no national bubble but that some markets showed signs of froth. Testimony before the Joint Economic Committee, June 9, 2005.

[16] "Realtors' economist rates area 'very healthy'" The Post and Courier, July 18, 2005, p. F8.

[17] Bureau of Labor Statistics, Series ID LASST25000003.

[18] Many lenders now sell their mortgages to investors in the secondary market reducing exposure to rising interest rates.

[19] Alternative Mortgages Parity Act, 1982. 12 U.S.C. sec. 3801.

[20] Federal Housing Finance Board, 2006 Mortgage Market Statistical Annual - Volume 1, p. 17.

[21] The FHFB combines some MSAs for reporting purposes so there is not an exact match with the OFHEO price index.

[22] Economic Real Estate Trends, Fall 2006 p. 7. The index is published by the PMI Group which sells private mortgage insurance.

[23] Statistical analysis of the share of ARMs and the risk index shows a positive and significant correlation. [coefficient =9.2, t-stat =5.7, R-Squared = 0.72, df=30].

[24] OFHEO News Release, November 30, 2006.

[25] U.S. Home Prices: Does Bust Always Follow Boom?, FDIC, February 10, 2005.

In: Understanding Mortgage Meltdowns
Editor: A. V. Carey ISBN: 978-1-60692-789-2

Chapter 3

ECONOMIC ANALYSIS OF A MORTGAGE FORECLOSURE MORATORIUM*

Edward Vincent Murphy

ABSTRACT

On July 26, 2008, Congress passed legislation creating a voluntary program to enable troubled mortgage borrowers and lenders to refinance their loans through the Federal Housing Administration (FHA). Having created the voluntary program, it remains to be seen if people will be willing and able to participate under current financial market conditions. Meanwhile, the pace of foreclosures continues to rise, even as another category of loans, Alt-A, approaches the peak of its payment resets. The foreclosure process may be costly and cumbersome. Some have argued for a moratorium on foreclosures to give distressed borrowers and lenders time to seek financial relief. Others might argue that delaying foreclosures may also delay the recapitalization of the banking system and ultimately delay restoration of stability in financial markets. Proponents might counter that providing additional time to keep current borrowers in their homes will ultimately reduce the magnitude of bank losses and lessen the need for recapitalization.

The persistence of large unsold inventories of housing may be an indicator that house prices may fall further. Further declines in house prices might contribute to more foreclosures and more instability in financial

* This is an edited, excerpted and augmented edition of a Congressional Research Service Publication RL34653, dated September 12, 2008.

markets. Although economists generally believe that prices adjust to clear shortages and surpluses, it could be argued that the housing market has characteristics that make that process longer and more painful than in some other consumer goods markets. In housing markets, several factors may contribute to a feedback loop (where housing market instability becomes self-reinforcing). Potential obstructions to price adjustment and market clearing in the housing market include builders hesitating to lower prices for new houses because they may have duties to previous customers; the reluctance or inability of some homeowners to sell their houses for less than they owe on their current mortgages; the addition of foreclosures to housing supply when prices fall; the tendency of some potential buyers to wait for market prices to hit bottom; and the reduction of available mortgage credit during a housing market downturn.

A moratorium would have costs and benefits. On the benefit side, it would provide all market participants with more time to assess asset prices and evaluate alternatives. On the cost side, it could delay the ability of markets to clear excess inventories and restore financial stability. Evidence from the Great Depression suggests that states that enacted moratoriums provided relief to some home owners but saw higher costs of credit and fewer loans compared with states that did not. It nevertheless has been argued that natural disasters are an appropriate analogy and that the oncoming schedule of Alt-A mortgage resets creates time pressure that, in the absence of a moratorium, could overwhelm the capacity of loan servicers.

A regulatory foreclosure freeze has been announced by the FDIC for IndyMac loans. Some have called for a foreclosure freeze for loans held by the GSEs in conservatorship. In Congress, H.R. 6076 would set up a deferment period during which home owners would make a payment calculated by formula.

This report will be updated as conditions warrant.

BACKGROUND

On July 26, 2008, Congress passed legislation creating a voluntary program to enable troubled mortgage borrowers and lenders to refinance their loans through the Federal Housing Administration (FHA).[1] Having created the voluntary program, it remains to be seen if people will be willing and able to participate under current financial market conditions. Meanwhile, the pace of foreclosures continues to rise, even as another category of loans, Alt-A, approaches the peak of its payment resets.[2] The foreclosure process may be costly and cumbersome.[3] Some have argued for a moratorium on foreclosures to give distressed borrowers and lenders time to seek financial relief. Others might argue that delaying foreclosures may also delay the recapitalization of the banking system and ultimately delay restoration of stability in financial markets. Proponents might counter that providing additional time to keep current borrowers in their homes will ultimately reduce the magnitude of bank losses and lessen the need for recapitalization.

There have been calls to delay or freeze mortgage foreclosures. H.R. 6076, the Home Retention and Economic Stabilization Act of 2008, was introduced by Representative Matsui on May 15, 2008.[4] This bill would grant delinquent subprime and negative amortization borrowers up to an additional 270 days prior to foreclosure. On the regulatory side, the FDIC has announced that it will halt foreclosures for loans that it administers through its supervision of IndyMac Bank, which recently failed.[5] Some have reportedly called for the recent conservatorship of Fannie Mae and Freddie Mac to freeze foreclosures for the loans that these institutions hold.[6]

Economic Analysis of Delaying Foreclosure

Delaying foreclosure could have benefits. Borrowers who may not have fully prepared for payment increases built into their mortgages would have more time to adjust their household finances. They would also have more time to consider participating in the newly enacted voluntary program to refinance loans into FHA at reduced principal, if their lenders agreed. Similarly, lenders would have more time to consider loan modification, or participation in the new FHA program, as a loss- minimizing alternative to the costly foreclosure process, especially considering the decline in the value of houses, which serve as collateral for the loans. Other home owners trying to sell their homes would not have to compete with quite so many foreclosure sales, which often drive down prices. Neighborhoods and communities might be able to slow the growth of concentrated pockets of vacant and poorly maintained homes, which sometimes become magnets for accidents, crime, and even breeding grounds for disease carrying pests.[7]

The benefits for some of a delay could come at a cost to others. Renters who may desire to purchase a home but were priced out during the previous housing boom might have fewer opportunities than they would without a foreclosure deferment program. Some banks, who are already experiencing liquidity and solvency problems, would lose at least one potential avenue of recapitalization (selling the collateral of under-performing loans). It is possible that a deferment plan could simply delay the bottoming out of the housing market and extend the period of large unsold housing inventories, in which case potential buyers who are waiting for prices to trough might remain on the sidelines. If the return of potential home buyers were delayed on a large scale then it would be possible that mortgage markets and related financial institutions might remain in turmoil for an extended period, disrupting the financing of student loans, auto leases, municipal funding, and other seemingly unrelated markets.

Trade-offs, such as the potential benefits and costs of foreclosure deferment, are central to the economic approach. Although competitive markets are said to allocate resources efficiently (under certain assumptions), the persistence of large unsold inventories of houses is not consistent with a market in equilibrium.[8] Rapid declines in house prices have not as yet drawn buyers back in on a large scale. In economic theory, the ability of private actors to effectively evaluate trade-offs and reach efficient outcomes depends upon transaction costs, the availability of relevant information, and the presence of competing buyers and sellers.[9] These theoretical conditions for economic efficiency can be useful for diagnosing potential obstacles to private bargaining solutions.

The central trade-off in evaluating a deferment is the cost and benefits of quickly moving the ownership of assets from distressed hands to secure hands. Many observers recognize that delays in reallocation has opportunity costs: at least some of the policy considerations in bankruptcy are intended to facilitate this asset transfer and minimize the costs of delay. But economists recognize that speed itself has costs; for example, two researchers of financial crises have observed that "... speed can actually work against a well-functioning procedure if time is required to properly assess the value of assets and claims, allow for negotiations, search for potential bidders, and generally increase the liquidity of the bidding process."[10] From an economic perspective, analysis of a moratorium on foreclosures in the current housing cycle focuses on the factors that could affect the speed of reducing the inventory of unsold homes, including the uncertainty faced by market participants.

THE ECONOMICS OF EXCESS INVENTORIES IN THE HOUSING MARKET

In a relatively free market, prices are expected to adjust up or down to eliminate surpluses and shortages. Persistent surpluses, such as excess inventories of unsold homes, are often a sign that quantity supplied at the current price is greater than quantity demanded. In the current housing market, the inventory of unsold homes in many formerly appreciating markets is far above the historic average, an indicator that prices could fall further.[11] The expectation of further price declines could itself discourage new buyers and delay the restoration of more normal conditions.

Supply and Demand

The recent fall in house prices in formerly booming areas was not a random event that no one could have predicted; rather, a period of rising prices followed by a period of falling prices is the expected economic outcome when demand for a good rises and suppliers are delayed in their ability to respond to the increased profits (although it is often difficult to determine the timing and magnitude of price changes). That is, the increased demand initially bids up prices and increases producer profits, but eventually producers are able to increase capacity. Prices are then expected to fall back to reflect producer costs. This basic supply and demand approach is consistent with the recent experience of many formerly booming housing markets, including in Florida, California, Nevada, and Arizona. That is not to say that the housing market does not have various features that affect the speed by which house prices reduce shortages and surpluses; for example, producers must comply with zoning restrictions, and home purchasers are typically restricted by the availability of mortgage credit.

From an economist's point of view, the good news is that we do not have to wait for a random shock for the housing market to recover; rather, the market is expected to recover as (1) producers reduce construction (which has already happened in many areas), (2) normal demographic household formation increases the number of potential home purchasers, and (3) price declines bring affordable home ownership within the reach of a greater percentage of an area's population. The combination of fewer housing units for sale and more potential home buyers will eventually stabilize the housing market. From the point of view of many policymakers, however, the bad news is that this process may take longer, and the amount of dislocation caused may be greater, because of several features of the mortgage market — features that may be subject to amelioration. Five factors may tend to prolong surpluses of unsold homes and delay the stabilization of housing markets: builder attitudes toward prior home buyers, nominal mortgage contracts, foreclosure supply feedbacks, potential buyers waiting for prices to bottom out, and financial problems of the providers of mortgage funds, such as banks and government-sponsored enterprises (GSEs). A moratorium on foreclosure could potentially address some, but not all, of these factors.

Attitude of Developers toward Prior Home Purchasers

Home builders who develop large neighborhoods are often reluctant to lower prices because this can anger earlier buyers. Rather than lower the asking price of the home, the builder might prefer to offer other incentives, such as reduced financing costs or discounted options (such as granite countertops or a jacuzzi tub). Because builders may raise prices when conditions allow but seek alternatives to recording price declines when conditions are reversed, a period of slowing sales may occur rather than a period of falling prices. As a result, potential buyers may not know that the real cost of homes has fallen into their price range and other sellers (such as owners of existing homes) may not realize that they will be unlikely to find a buyer if they do not lower their asking price. This reluctance of builders to lower asking prices was observed earlier in the housing cycle but many builders have since capitulated.

In the current housing cycle, builder reliance on financing incentives and construction options rather than price reductions is probably no longer a significant obstacle to the clearance of unsold inventories. Builders began aggressively cutting prices and trying to clear their own inventories in many areas earlier in the housing cycle. Builders have also reduced new construction, as measured by housing starts, and have cancelled, or failed to exercise, many of their options on land for development. A moratorium on foreclosures would be unlikely to affect the incentives of builders to try to avoid lowering asking prices.

Nominal Mortgage Contracts, Inflation,and Sticky House Prices

Prices that are not adjusted for inflation are called nominal prices. The vast majority of mortgages do not directly adjust the monthly payment for changes in the inflation rate. Because the United States has generally experienced inflation since World War II, most Americans have had the real (as opposed to nominal) price reflected in their monthly mortgage payment decline over time. Similarly, inflation has masked periods of declining real house prices. Nominal house prices continued rising in some areas even though the real prices of houses declined once inflation was taken into account. In individual cities, even nominal house prices had been known to fall, sometimes sharply. The claim that the United States as a whole has not experienced a house price decline is not true for real house prices.

The distinction between nominal and real prices is important. First, some Americans may have been overconfident that the price of their home would never decline. As a result, they may have accepted mortgage terms that would commit them to refinancing their houses quickly even if they could only do so if house prices continued climbing. Consistent with this analysis, the use of mortgages with low down payments and low introductory monthly payments is concentrated in areas that formerly had rapid price appreciation. Now the default and delinquency rate on these loans, for all classes of borrowers, has risen significantly. The wave of payment resets caused by the expiration of these introductory periods in areas in which the expected appreciation did not occur is one of the reasons that some policymakers wish to quickly facilitate mortgage refinances.

The second reason why the nominal mortgage contract is important is because it may create an obstacle to clearing the unsold housing inventory. A homeowner who cannot make the current monthly mortgage payment can avoid foreclosure by selling the house as long as there is positive equity in the home. Falling house prices reduce the homeowner's equity; in some areas prices have fallen enough that many recent home purchasers, even prime borrowers, now have negative equity. A person cannot sell his or her home to avoid foreclosure if he or she does not have adequate equity or sufficient savings to pay off the current creditor and any other selling costs, such as the real estate agent. Unless the lender agrees to accept less than the amount owed on the original loan (e.g., a short sale), there is a nominal price floor below which these homeowners cannot go — a price floor prolongs an economic surplus, such as the inventory of unsold homes. Historically, it was common for distressed debtors to advocate for greater inflation, which is consistent with a desire to lower the real price when it is difficult to lower the nominal price.

A moratorium on foreclosures could affect nominal mortgage contracts because it would increase the length of time that inflation can affect real house prices. That being said, the current inflation rate is significantly below the magnitude that is probably necessary to lower real house prices enough that prospective buyers could meet many sellers' nominal price floors. The inflation rate as measured by the consumer price index from July 2007 to July 2008 was 5.6%, which is significantly less than nominal price declines in some areas.[12] For example, the nominal price decline for San Francisco measured by the Case Schiller home price index from May 2007 to May 2008 was -23%.[13] If inflation is included, the real price declined even further. Another example, from an alternative measure of housing prices from the Office of Federal Housing Enterprise Oversight (OFHEO), which is generally less volatile than the Case Schiller index, reported a nominal price decline in Sacramento, CA, of -13.2%.[14] Because it would take two to three years for the current rate of inflation to compensate for even one year's nominal price decline in some areas, it is unlikely that a brief moratorium on foreclosures would significantly reduce that part of the impediment to equilibrium that is caused by the use of nominal prices in mortgage contracts.

Foreclosures and Unmanageable Resets Increase Supply

There are some problems in housing markets that create a feedback loop that can increase the number of homes being offered for sale when prices are falling. In areas where the direction of prices unexpectedly switches from rising to falling, for example, people who counted on further price appreciation to enable them to refinance their homes on more favorable terms will be frustrated, and some may try to sell their homes to avoid foreclosure.[15] Price reductions also increase the number of home owners who owe more than their home is worth, especially if there have been a large number of buyers who put little or nothing down. The combination of home owners who cannot afford a scheduled increase in their monthly mortgage payments and those who no longer have sufficient incentive to continue paying down a loan because their negative equity is large (more than $100,000 in some areas) tends to increase the number of homes offered for sale in precisely those areas that once had rapid price increases but are now experiencing rapid price declines. Although the peak period of payment resets for subprime mortgages reportedly is passing, other mortgages with a reset feature (e.g., so-called Alt-A and Hybrid ARMs) that are even more highly concentrated in formerly rapidly appreciating regions will be triggered in 2008, 2009, and 2010.[16] The net result is that falling house prices can also increase supply (over some range) through a feedback process between negative equity and default rates.

A foreclosure moratorium may, under some circumstances, help to reduce the supply feedback effect of falling house prices. In the short run, it would slow down the number of distress sales in the marketplace and reduce the downward pressure on prices. Because foreclosure sales also affect the existing homeowners' perceptions of the value of their own homes, it could be argued that foreclosure sales increase the incentive of people to choose to default opportunistically when their negative equity is high.[17] On the other hand, negative equity is a necessary but not a sufficient condition for foreclosure (because a pre-foreclosure sale can avoid default if there is positive equity). One study of borrowers in Massachusetts with negative equity in the 1 990s, for example, found that more than 90% retained their homes, suggesting that opportunistic default may be overstated in some cases.[18]

A moratorium might also allow households that have unmanageable payment resets to adjust their household finances. Eligible families may be able to refinance into a more affordable loan or negotiate new terms with their existing creditors, perhaps by taking advantage of the new FHA program.[19] Some people who used mortgages with low introductory payments and were surprised when house prices failed to continue appreciating would have time to adjust both their expenses and their earnings. Household earnings can be raised in some cases, for example, by having a family member return to work or by renting a room to a boarder.[20] In some cases, there may be a delay between realization that a payment reset will be unaffordable and the family's ability to adjust earnings and expenses.

The effect of a moratorium on the supply feedback of foreclosures and unmanageable resets is hard to project. On the one hand, a delay in foreclosure is unlikely to reduce the incentive of people with large negative equity to opportunistically default. If these people will eventually default anyway then a moratorium merely delays the inevitable and extends the period of destabilizing unsold inventories. On the other hand, a delay in foreclosure could provide those families whose expectations of market conditions were frustrated and now face a large payment reset additional time to adjust their finances to new market realities. These families might avoid foreclosure altogether given extra time, which would tend to reduce the total supply feedback, both during the moratorium period and after its expiration.

Fence-Sitters, Potential Buyers May Wait for Prices to Bottom out

Just as price declines can cause a foreclosure supply feedback process that extends, rather than shortens, the period of large unsold inventories, price declines may also have a negative demand feedback effect by deterring potential buyers from entering the market. Buyers who believe that prices will continue to fall may decide to wait until the market bottoms out, yet by waiting as a group they have the cumulative effect of encouraging the price decline.[21] That is, expectations of a future price decline reduce the number of potential buyers at the current price (and all other prices), which has the effect of putting downward pressure on prices.

The effect of a moratorium on fence-sitters would depend on their expectations, which may be difficult to anticipate. If fence-sitters believe that a moratorium will be effective in stabilizing the housing market (perhaps there will be income growth for families, or wide scale refinances, or rapid inflation during the moratorium period), then fence sitters would gain little by waiting. On the other hand, if fence- sitters believe that a moratorium will merely delay inevitable distress sales then the moratorium could have the perverse effect of further discouraging fence-sitters from entering the market.

Financial Problems of Banks and GSEs Reduce Demand for Houses

The mortgage finance system is another factor that could tend to limit the ability of housing markets to restore equilibrium quickly. In the United States, the vast majority of home sales require mortgage financing so the supply of mortgage funds is a critical component of the demand for houses. Falling house prices create a negative feedback loop in the mortgage finance system because mortgage funds tend to dry up as housing markets decline. First, when housing prices are declining, lenders tighten lending standards and require larger downpayments to reduce the probability of negative equity and default because the decline in the value of the collateral (the house) increases the risk to the lender in the event of default. Second, the higher delinquency rate on existing loans that usually occurs concurrently with falling house prices also reduces the revenues of banks and other mortgage lenders. Because financial institutions that provide mortgage financing are typically leveraged (they have liabilities that are many times their capital), the failure of existing borrowers to repay their loans can force the lenders to curtail new lending by a multiple of the lost revenue. As a result, the ability of potential house buyers to obtain financing can be reduced when prices fall, which can further reduce prices. In the current housing market downturn, the financial condition of many mortgage lenders and related financial institutions, such as Fannie Mae and Freddie Mac, is significantly troubled.[22]

A moratorium on foreclosures is unlikely to help mortgage lenders, except those that might wish to modify loans on a wide scale but are uncertain whether and under what terms they may legally do so.[23] For those lenders and loan servicers with unencumbered ownership of their loans, they already have the option of delaying foreclosure proceedings. One reason for not delaying foreclosure is that the declining housing market is already eroding their capital position and the inability to recover any funds from a loan exacerbates their problems.[24]

It is difficult to assess the effect of a moratorium on the factors that tend to frustrate stabilization in the housing market. In some cases, such as the reaction of fence-sitters and financial institutions, it depends on expectations and calculations that policymakers may not be able to anticipate. The primary economic benefit of a moratorium, in terms of facilitating a return to equilibrium in the housing market, is that it gives market participants time to evaluate relevant information, such as the existence of new programs and the completion of new appraisals, after which existing borrowers and lenders may reconsider their options and negotiating positions. The next section focuses on the uncertainty in the current housing market.

Uncertainty Affecting Housing Market Participants

Uncertainty is one of the factors contributing to continued instability in mortgage markets and the financial system. It is difficult in the present circumstances to know if loan servicers have the capacity to conduct effective loss mitigation, including alternatives to foreclosure, in the face of rapidly rising delinquency rates and falling house prices. Press releases by the HOPE Now Alliance, a coalition of loan servicers and counselors, list hundreds of thousands of loan workouts but it is difficult to know if these are actions merely begun or actions completed.[25]

Loan Servicers

Uncertainty about the value of houses in declining markets, for example, complicates the ability of loan servicers to evaluate the returns to loan modification compared with completing the foreclosure process. Similarly, uncertainty about home values also complicates the funding of new loans that could serve to bring buyers back into the marketplace because lenders generally raise qualification standards and down payment requirements if they believe house prices might fall after the loan is finalized.[26]

In addition to uncertainty about the value of homes, loan servicers had a period of uncertainty with regard to the extent of their discretion to modify loans in anticipation of payment problems. Innovations in financial services had allowed for a fracturing of ownership of the loans with the result that there was not a single lender to authorize changes in loss mitigation strategies. This may have resulted in over-reliance on loan-by-loan loss mitigation efforts instead of greater use of broad- based action for loan categories experiencing delinquencies on a large scale. Over the past year, some of this uncertainty has been reduced by a series of industry standards, Securities and Exchange Commission (SEC) announcements, and Internal Revenue Service (IRS) rulings.[27] Given these recent developments, it is difficult to establish the accuracy of statements by HOPE Now that loan modifications are proceeding at an increased pace.

Borrowers

Borrowers must acquire information about their alternatives. Although there have been outreach efforts, many borrowers might not respond to loan servicers even when the servicers may be willing to renegotiate more lenient terms. Similarly, many borrowers may not be aware of the existence of the new voluntary FHA refinance program or if their lenders might be willing to participate. Even if they know of the existence of the program, they may not know if they qualify, or under what terms. For example, the new program requires the new loan balance to be reduced to 90% of the current appraised value, but no one can know the current appraised value without conducting a new appraisal. Without knowing this new balance, troubled borrowers may not be able to accurately assess their own ability to meet the new monthly payments and so may not know if they themselves would be willing to participate in the new program.

Lenders

Just as borrowers require information to assess their alternatives, lenders might require information to assess their alternatives. Before deciding to participate in the new FHA program, lenders also need information on current house prices, as determined by a host of new appraisals. The shelf-life of an estimate of an area's house prices might not be very long in areas with rapidly declining prices; therefore, it may be difficult, at least on a large scale, to get information on current house prices to determine new balances under the voluntary FHA program.

Depending on their assessment of house prices, banks may wish to pursue their own broad-based alternatives, such as the one put forward by the Federal Deposit Insurance Corporation (FDIC), rather than participate in the new FHA program, even if the banks decide to forgo the foreclosure process.[28] Similarly, the willingness of banks to lend to new customers in an area depends on the bank's changing perception of the area.

Foreclosure Moratoriums in Historical Perspective

Although inflation-adjusted house prices have occasionally fallen in the past 30 years, nominal house prices have not fallen on a national scale since before OFHEO began collecting house price data in the late 1970s (falling house prices on a national scale was more common prior to World War II). In part because inflation generally adds to the home equity of borrowers with traditional 30-year fixed rate mortgages and holds down foreclosure rates, it has been several generations since there has been a call for a mortgage moratorium on a national scale. There have been localized programs for natural disasters (the aftermath of Hurricanes Katrina and Rita is an example) in recent years, and there were national efforts prior to World War II. The following section discusses historical examples of mortgage moratoriums.

Great Depression

The Great Depression saw falling asset prices along with growing, and persistent, unsold inventories for many commodities and for farm mortgages. The magnitude of the problem during the Great Depression was far greater than problems in the current housing market but some of the same basic economic principles of housing markets, mortgage defaults, unsold inventories, and financial turmoil might still apply. Prior to becoming chairman of the Federal Reserve, Ben Bernanke was a recognized expert on the economic connection between mortgage defaults and broader credit market turmoil during the Great Depression. Evidence of the effect of state mortgage moratoriums during the period is found in the work of economist Lee Alston. The following sections describe, for the Great Depression, the supposed feedback loop between mortgage defaults and financial market turmoil, reported efforts of market participants to address unsold inventories, and economic analysis of the mortgage moratoriums during the period.

Mortgage Defaults and Financial Turmoil Feedback in the 193 0s. In drawing lessons from the Great Depression, Bernanke says that a "...major aspect of the financial crisis (one that is currently neglected by historians) was the pervasiveness of debtor insolvency. Given that debt contracts were written in nominal terms, the protracted fall in prices and money greatly increased debt burdens."[29] Bernanke goes on to explain how debtor insolvency also caused problems for lenders, contributed to a banking crisis, and ultimately damaged the ability of financial markets to provide credit intermediation. In Bernanke's analysis, when a wave of insolvencies causes a big shock to the lending system, the cost of credit intermediation (the ability to distinguish "good" borrowers from "bad" borrowers)[30] rises and provides a separate, nonmonetary channel, through which problems in the banking sector can negatively affect the real economy. Bernanke cites Depression-era sources who say "...that the extraordinary rate of default on residential mortgages forced banks and life insurance companies to practically stop making mortgage loans, except for renewals."[31] Bernanke concludes that economic institutions matter — that "institutions which evolve and perform well in normal times may become counterproductive during periods when exogenous shocks or policy mistakes drive the economy off course."

Some might consider the modern day rise and fall of the securitization of mortgages as another example of a shock to credit intermediation.[32] For example, Laura Kodres, division chief in the International Monetary Fund's Monetary and Capital Markets Department, is one of many critics of the "originate to distribute" model of mortgage finance. She attributes some of the lax underwriting during the boom to "Supervisors had insufficient information and clout to halt the proliferation of overpriced securities. Thus, competitive pressures to issue and sell these types of products were so intense that — as Charles Prince, Chairman and Chief Executive Officer of Citigroup, told a reporter in early July that year — top management felt that 'as long as the music is playing, you've got to get up and dance.'"[33] The securitization system, which appeared to work well during the housing boom, appears to have become counterproductive since housing markets have declined. Global collateralized debt obligation (CDO) issuance was 62% lower in the second half of 2007 than in the second half of 2006.[34] This decline in securitization occurred despite the Federal Reserve lowering the Fed Funds rate 25 basis points between August 2006 and August 2007.[35] Even borrowers with good credit are reporting problems in obtaining loans.

Efforts to Stabilize Markets by Preventing Price Declines

During the Great Depression, some believed that the way to recovery was to hold products off the market to slow down price declines, with some actions that in hindsight might seem perverse — farmers stopping their neighbors' milk wagons and dumping out the milk, for example.[36] Reducing inventory to support prices was also one of the justifications for paying farmers to reduce the amount of acreage under cultivation. Few observers believe that Depression-era price supports were effective in facilitating recovery of individual markets.[37] In the current housing market, there have been several efforts to reduce the number of properties for sale and support prices; for example, some state and local governments have programs to acquire foreclosed properties and the recently passed omnibus housing bill has provisions for Community Development Block Grant Funds to be used to acquire vacant properties.[38] A moratorium on foreclosures may give state and local governments more time to remove vacant properties to try to support prices.

Economic Analysis of Depression-Era Mortgage Moratoriums

Between 1932 and 1934, 25 states passed moratoriums on the foreclosure of mortgages. Economists might argue that interference with a lender's ability to recover loan collateral will tend to either reduce the amount of lending or raise interest rates on new loans. Economist Lee Alston examined the economic effects of the 1930s moratorium legislation. Alston found that some borrowers gained from the temporary reprieve, "but that this reprieve was at the expense of private creditors and prospective farmers who were precluded from securing credit to purchase a farm because of the increased costs to private creditors."[39] He arrived at this result by examining whether the quantity of private loans fell, or the interest rates on loans rose, in states that passed moratoriums relative to states that did not (controlling for other credit market factors). He found that the quantity of private loans fell and that interest rates rose under a variety of model specifications.

Criticism of the Depression Analogy

Some would argue that evidence from Depression-era moratoriums is not necessarily the best analogy. As discussed above, farm mortgages were often the primary source of family income so that falling commodity prices simultaneously reduced the value of the farm and the ability to make mortgage payments, unlike the present situation in which an individual household's income is largely divorced from house prices (although aggregate regional income may affect regional house prices). Similarly, Depression era efforts to support prices by reducing supply were largely directed at commodity prices, not house prices. Also, the basic macroeconomic policy approach to recovery, especially the modern bias toward inflation and expansionary monetary policy as a response to recessions, may make evidence from prior periods less relevant. Finally, institutions for financial markets have changed significantly (including greater reliance on global sources of funding and more alternatives for federal subsidies) since the Depression so Alston's evidence may apply to a system that is no longer in place. Finally, current moratoriums are being considered to give both borrowers and lenders more time to consider alternatives to foreclosure, not necessarily to stabilize housing prices; therefore, an example of time pressure may be more appropriate.

Natural Disasters

Sometimes when natural disasters hit, disruptions of traditional communications can add to the obvious difficulties of distressed residents to meet their mortgage payments on time. In these situations, it is not uncommon for there to be a temporary reprieve of debt obligations until normalcy can be restored. One example of this was a moratorium on foreclosures of FHA-insured mortgages in the aftermath of Hurricanes Katrina and Rita.[40] As in most natural disasters, the event that caused the communications disruption also reduced the ability of families to raise funds to pay their mortgages and destroyed some of the housing stock. In the case of Hurricanes Katrina and Rita, flooding reportedly damaged 1.2 million housing units. Of those, 300,000 were seriously damaged or destroyed.[41] The longterm impact on some communities was severe and in some cases out-migration may have permanently reduced the local population.[42] These shocks to both the supply and demand of housing have left an area that arguably remains in disequilibrium. The moratorium likely provided time for affected residents to determine if they wished to make a long-term commitment, such as home ownership, to the affected region.

Some aspects of the natural disaster analogy seem to fit the current housing market and some do not. If forecasts of the inability of many borrowers to meet higher payments after initial reset are accurate, then some would argue that the schedule of resetting mortgages represents an "approaching tsunami of mortgage defaults."[43] In this view, traditional avenues of communication between borrowers and servicers are inadequate to handle the volume of renegotiations necessary to modify loans prior to severe delinquency (most loans that become more than 90 days late never again become current). In part because of the time constraint, the FDIC has recommended simply writing down loan balances en masse to more affordable payments to keep current borrowers in their homes and prevent more housing units to be added to unsold inventory through the foreclosure process.[44]

On the other hand, the natural disaster analogy may not be appropriate. Unlike a natural disaster, neither the housing stock nor the communications network have been damaged beyond the control of market participants. Rather, borrowers in some cases avoid communications with loan servicers who try to contact them. Similarly, some loan servicers might try to contact borrowers but then avoid negotiating more lenient terms both because it might make it more likely that other borrowers will seek more lenient terms (borrowers who do not necessarily have an affordability problem) and because a reputation for lowering balances may be bad for bidding for future loan servicing contracts. Unlike in a natural disaster, it could be argued that borrowers and lenders are in a position to bargain.

Other Examples

The Great Depression and Hurricanes Katrina and Rita are arguably the two extremes — an extreme macroeconomic collapse on the one hand and extreme natural disasters on the other. The historical record of moratoriums on debt collections is extensive. For example, the May 1933 edition of the Harvard Law Review contains a comparative study of moratorium legislation.[45] Historic examples include a court case of Demosthenes regarding a general prohibition on debt collection actions against Greek soldiers away at war, a general moratorium decreed by the Emperor Justinian when the Franks invaded Italy and Sicily, and many other moratoriums during wars. Providing a moratorium on debt recovery has not been confined to periods of war; many U.S. states attempted to provide moratoriums during times of economic stress in the 1 800s. Excluding war years, the article lists 20 instances in which states tried to impose moratoriums on debt collections. Many of these attempts by states were found to be unconstitutional, but such restrictions would not necessarily apply to the federal government.

REFERENCES

[1] Passed as H.R. 3221, Housing and Economic Recovery Act of 2008, and enacted as P.L. 110-289 on July 30, 2008. See CRS Report RL34623, *Housing and Economic Recovery Act of 2008*, by N. Eric Weiss, Darryl E. Getter, Mark Jickling, Mark P. Keightley, Edward Vincent Murphy, and Bruce E. Foote.

[2] See CRS Report RL33775, Alternative Mortgages: Causes and Policy Implications of Troubled Mortgage Resets in the Subprime and Alt-A Markets, by Edward Vincent Murphy.

[3] See CRS Report RL34232, *Understanding Mortgage Foreclosure: Recent Events, the Process, and Costs*, by Darryl E. Getter, discussing estimates of foreclosure costs.

[4] See CRS Report RS22943, H.R. 6076: Home Retention and Economic Stabilization Act of 2008, by Edward V. Murphy.

[5] Federal Deposit Insurance Corporation, "Loan Modification Program for Distressed Indymac Mortgage Loans," press release, August 20, 2008, available at [http://www.fdic.gov/consumers/loans/ modification/ indymac.html].

[6] "Democrats call on Fannie, Freddie to halt foreclosures," Los Angeles Times online, September 12, 2008, available at [http://www.latimes. com/business/la-fi-fannie 12-2008sep 12,0, 1383031.story].

[7] Reportedly, vacant homes with pools that have not been maintained have become breeding grounds for mosquitos capable of carrying viruses. Blair Robertson, "Mosquito District Treats more Abandoned Pools: Homeowners in Foreclosure or Who Feel Financially Squeezed are a Likely Factor as Workers Fight West Nile Transmission," *Sacramento Bee*, July 8, 2008, p.B3.

[8] The National Association of Realtors reports that the unsold inventory of homes, expressed as the number of months required to sell all homes for sale at the current sales pace, is above 11 months supply. A more normal supply would be five to six months. Available at [http://www.realtor.org/press_room/news_releases/2008/ehs _down _injune].

[9] More formally known as the Coase Theorem, private bargaining is likely to reach economically efficient outcomes when property rights are well defined, transaction costs are zero, all necessary information is available, and prices reflect opportunity costs (as in competitive markets). Economic

efficiency is usually defined as the state in which it is no longer possible to rearrange resources to make one person better off without making someone else worse off (Pareto Standard), or alternatively efficiency is when all possible moves in which the gains to winners are larger than the losses to losers are taken advantage of (Kaldor-Hicks Standard).

[10] David Smith and Per Stromberg, "Maximizing the Value of Distressed Assets: Bankruptcy Law and the Efficient Reorganization of Firms," Chapter 8 of *Systemic Financial Crises*, Patrick Honohan and Luc Laeven editors (Cambridge: Cambridge University Press, 2005), p. 271.

[11] The National Association of Realtors report 11 months supply. Available at [http://www.realtor.org/research/research/ecoindicator]. Note the emphasis on the term "excess" inventory; the existence of at least some unsold inventory can be a healthy sign because it means consumers have a variety of choices.

[12] Unadjusted twelve month calculation, Bureau of Labor Statistics, July 2008, available at [http://www.bls.gov/news.release/pdf/cpi.pdf].

[13] Calculated from May 2007 to May 2008 from Standard and Poor's Case Schiller Price Index, available at [http://www2.standardandpoors.com/spf/pdf/index/CSHomePrice _History _072943 .xls].

[14] Calculated from OFHEO's house price index data from first quarter 2007 to first quarter 2008, not seasonally adjusted, available at [http://www.ofheo.gov/media/hpi/ 1 q08hpi_cbsa.csv].

[15] See CRS Report RL33775, Alternative Mortgages: Causes and Policy Implications of Troubled Mortgage Resets in the Subprime and Alt-A Markets, by Edward Vincent Murphy.

[16] Christopher Cagan, "Mortgage Payment Reset," Presentation at the Real Estate Research Council of Southern California, May 30, 2007, available at [http://www.csupomona.edu/ ~rerc/RERCSC%20 Chris% 20Cagan% 205.30.07.pdf].

[17] See CRS Report RL34232, Understanding Mortgage Foreclosure: Recent Events, the Process, and Costs, by Darryl E. Getter.

[18] Christopher L. Foote, Kristopher Gerardi, and Paul S. Willen, "Negative Equity and Foreclosure: Theory and Evidence," Federal Reserve Bank of Boston, Working Paper No. 08-3, available at [http://www.bos.frb.org/economic/ppdp/2008/ppdp0803.htm].

[19] A fact sheet for the FHA Secure program can be found at [http://portal.hud.gov/portal/page?_pageid=73,3 947211 &_dad= portal&_ schema=PORTAL].

[20] One press report of households trying to adapt to avoid foreclosure is Kareem Fahim and Ron Nixon, "Behind Newark Foreclosure Data, Ruined Credit and Crushed Hopes," *New York Times*, Mar 28, 2007, p. A1.

[21] Reportedly, home builders believe there are a number of potential first time home buyers who are waiting for house prices to reach their bottom. See Rex Nutting, "Single-family home starts drop to 17-year low," *Marketwatch*, July 17, 2008, available at [http : //www.marketwatch.com/news/story/single-family-home-starts-drop- 17-year/story.aspx?guid=%7BB9547567-8849-4400-9F8F-9A576 1A0D99F%7D].

[22] See CRS Report RL3466 1, *Fannie Mae's and Freddie Mac's Financial Problems: Frequently Asked Questions*, by N. Eric Weiss. The Treasury and the Federal Housing Finance Agency placed the GSEs in conservatorship on September 5, 2008.

[23] See CRS Report RL34372, The HOPE NOW Alliance/American Securitization Forum (ASF) Plan to Freeze Certain Mortgage Interest Rates, by David H. Carpenter and Edward Vincent Murphy.

[24] Despite having greater than minimum capital, banks and thrifts are having to set aside increasingly large loan loss reserves. "Testimony of John Reich, Director of the Office of Thrift Supervision, before The Senate Committee on Banking, Housing, and Urban Affairs," June 5, 2008, p. 3, available at [http://files.ots.treas.gov/87 1 66.pdf].

[25] Prior to the December 2007 HOPE Now mortgage freeze plan, the Conference of State Bank Supervisors (CSBS) did an analysis of HOPE Now data and found that HOPE Now had not distinguished between loss mitigation begun and loss mitigation completed. Only a small percentage of the borrowers listed by HOPE Now had completed a new workout plan. See State Foreclosure Prevention Working Group, April 2008, at [http://www.csbs.org/Content/NavigationMenu/Home/StateForeclosureApril2 008.pdf].

[26] *Supervisory Insights*, FDIC, Summer 2008. Banks are reminded to tighten lending standards in declining markets for commercial real estate sector. Similar principles apply to the residential sector. Available

at [http://www.fdic.gov/regulations/examinations/ supervisory/ insights/ sisum08/ sisum08.pdf].

[27] See CRS Report RL34372, The HOPE NOW Alliance/American Securitization Forum (ASF) Plan to Freeze Certain Mortgage Interest Rates, by David H. Carpenter and Edward Vincent Murphy.

[28] The FDIC instituted its own wide scale loan modification plan for the borrowers it deals with when it took over IndyMac Bank. Details of the FDIC plan can be found at [http://www.fdic.gov/consumers/ loans/modification/indymac.html].

[29] Ben Bernanke, "Nonmonetary Effects of the Financial Crisis," *American Economic Review*, vol. 73 (June 1983).

[30] In this context, "good" and "bad" refer to the likelihood that borrowers will repay the loan.

[31] Bernanke citing Hart, *Debts and Recovery, 1929-1937*, New York, Twentieth Century Fund, 1938, p. 163. Renewals were similar to a refinance. Many mortgages prior to WWII were for short periods, often five years or less, with a large balloon payment at the end. As a result, people would have to roll over their mortgage at regular intervals.

[32] See CRS Report RS22722, Securitization and Federal Regulation of Mortgages for Safety and Soundness, by Edward Vincent Murphy.

[33] Laura Kodres, "A Crisis of Confidence... and a Lot More," Finance and Development, IMF, June 2008, available at [http://www.imf.org/external/ pubs/ft/fandd/2008/06/ kodres.htm#author].

[34] *SIFMA Research Quarterly*, February 2008, p. 8, available at [http://www.sifma.org/ research/pdf/RRVol3-2.pdf].

[35] Federal reserve historical data, available at [http://www.federalr eserve.gov/releases/h1 5/ data/Monthly/H1 5_FF_O .txt].

[36] For one personal story of the Farm Holiday movement, see the interview of Harry Terrell in Studs Terkel, *Hard Times: An Oral History of the Great Depression*, Pantheon Books, New York, 1970, pp. 2 13-217. For a discussion of policies to prevent further price declines, including the "plow up the pigs" campaigns, see *Depression Decade: From New Era through New Deal*, 1929-1941 (New York, Rinehart & Co., 1947), pp. 191-197.

[37] Other approaches to market stabilization were tried during the Great Depression, which may have been more effective. For a discussion of one such program, the Home Owner's Loan Corporation, see CRS Report RL34423, *Government Interventions in Financial Markets:*

Economic and Historic Analysis of Subprime Mortgage Options, by N. Eric Weiss.

[38] The Ohio Foreclosure Prevention Task Force, for example, recommended the use of authority under delinquent tax rules for communities to seize properties and in some cases demolish vacant houses. *Final Report*, September 10, 2007, p. 23, available at [http://www.com.state.oh.us/admn/pub/FinalReport.pdf].

[39] Lee J. Alston, "Farm Foreclosure Moratorium Legislation: A Lesson from the Past," *American Economic Review*, June, 1984, pp. 445-457.

[40] HUD repeatedly extended forbearance and a moratorium on FHA insured mortgage foreclosures in the Hurricane affected region. See for example, Mortgagee Letter 2006-05, February 3, 2006, available at [http://www.hud.gov/offices/adm/hudclips/letters/mortgagee/files/06-05 ML.doc].

[41] See CRS Report RL34087, FEMA Disaster Housing and Hurricane Katrina: Overview, Analysis, and Congressional Issues, by Francis X. McCarthy and CRS Report RL33 173, Hurricane Katrina: Questions Regarding the Section 8 Housing Voucher Program, by Maggie McCarty.

[42] Louisiana's Road Home Program, for example, had difficulty complying with federal law because it proposed to adjust aid based on the ability to own in three years, with an exemption for elderly people planning to leave the state. Some of the other assistance funds, including federal Community Development Block Grant Funds, were used to turn some former housing units into green space. See "Testimony of Gil Jamieson," Deputy Director of Gulf Coast Recovery, Federal Emergency Management Administration, before the House Financial Services Committee, February 22, 2007, p. 6.

[43] Concern over the capacity of servicers to meet loan modification efforts has been a subject of ongoing congressional concern. For example, the House Financial Services Committee held a hearing on July 25, 2008, entitled "A Review of Mortgage Servicing Practices and Foreclosure Mitigation." The tsunami analogy has made its way into media coverage, for example, Christopher Hayes, "The Coming Foreclosure Tsunami," *The Nation*, November 13, 2007

[44] The FDIC implemented its own variation on this plan when it took over IndyMac Bank. The FDIC is trying to contact IndyMac's delinquent borrowers to offer to write down their loans to a 38% debt-to-income

level. Information on the FDIC plan is available at [http://www.fdic.gov/news/news/press/2008/pr08067.html].

[45] See A.H. Feller, "Moratory Legislation: A Comparative Study," 46:7 *Harvard Law Review*, May 1933, pp. 1061-1085.

In: Understanding Mortgage Meltdowns
Editor: A. V. Carey
ISBN: 978-1-60692-789-2

Chapter 4

UNDERSTANDING MORTGAGE FORECLOSURE: RECENT EVENTS, THE PROCESS, AND COSTS*

Darryl E. Getter

ABSTRACT

As evidenced by the numerous bills introduced in the 110th Congress during the first session, there is much concern over recent developments in the housing and mortgage markets. Bills such as H.R. 3019, the Expand and Preserve Home Ownership Through Counseling Act (Representative Judy Biggert), and H.R. 3666, the Foreclosure Prevention and Home Ownership Protection Act (Representative Betty Sutton et al.), include sections that speak specifically about foreclosures. These bills would authorize studies on current defaults and foreclosures, as well as possible causes. In addition, H.R. 5818, the Neighborhood Stabilization Act of 2008 (Representative Maxine Waters), has been introduced to establish a loan and grant program, administered by the Department of Housing and Urban Development, to help states purchase and rehabilitate foreclosed homes to stabilize as many properties as possible. This report provides a general analysis and overview of current foreclosure issues addressed in the bills cited above.

---

* This is an edited, excerpted and augmented edition of a Congressional Research Service Publication RL34232, dated April 18, 2008.

It begins with a description of the behavior of aggregate foreclosure rates. The behaviors of foreclosure rates are placed in the context of activity in the housing and mortgage market to illustrate any relationships. The foreclosure process is then explained, first from the point of view of a traditional financial lending institution, and then from the viewpoint of securitization when loans are sold in secondary markets. Finally, this report collects information from other studies to obtain an estimate of the average foreclosure costs. A brief discussion of the effect uniform foreclosure legislation may have on costs follows.

INTRODUCTION

The recent rise in mortgage foreclosure rates may warrant a more detailed understanding of the foreclosure process, which is the focus of this report. A brief summary of foreclosure activity and concurrent activity in the housing market begins the discussion. Next, a description of the foreclosure process is presented, first under a traditional banking context, followed by a summary of how the process works when mortgage loans are securitized. The last sections focus on lender foreclosure costs. Estimates of foreclosures costs are presented followed by a discussion of whether a national foreclosure law could help reduce those costs.

THE RECENT FORECLOSURE EXPERIENCE

The Mortgage Bankers Association (MBA) reports on the percentage of delinquencies and foreclosures in its National Delinquency Survey (NDS) every quarter. The sample consists of more than 41 million loans serviced by mortgage companies, commercial banks, thrifts, credit unions, and other servicing institutions.[1] The data on foreclosure rates used in Figure 1 and Figure 2 come from the NDS. The figures include data on foreclosure rates for prime loans, Federal Housing Administration (FHA) insured loans, subprime loans, and a composite rate for all foreclosed loans. The foreclosure rate for each loan category is computed as the total number of foreclosures at the end of the quarter divided by the total number of loans in that particular category. The loan categories are defined as follows:

Prime loans are typically made to creditworthy borrowers who meet the standards set by the government sponsored enterprises (GSEs) known as Fannie Mae or Freddie Mac.[2]
Alternative or "Alt-A" loans typically meet the GSE credit score requirements; however, they do not meet the standard requirements for documentation, property type, debt (or qualifying) ratios, or loanto-value (LTV) ratios. FHA targets Alt-A borrowers, although they do insure loans for borrowers with lower credit scores. Although the agency allows more flexibility with respect to debt and LTV ratios than prime lenders, FHA borrowers typically must comply with standard documentation requirements.
Subprime loans are made primarily to borrowers with impaired or limited credit. Subprime loans do not have to meet the GSE credit score requirements, and other standard underwriting requirements may also be waived, including standard documentation requirements.[3]

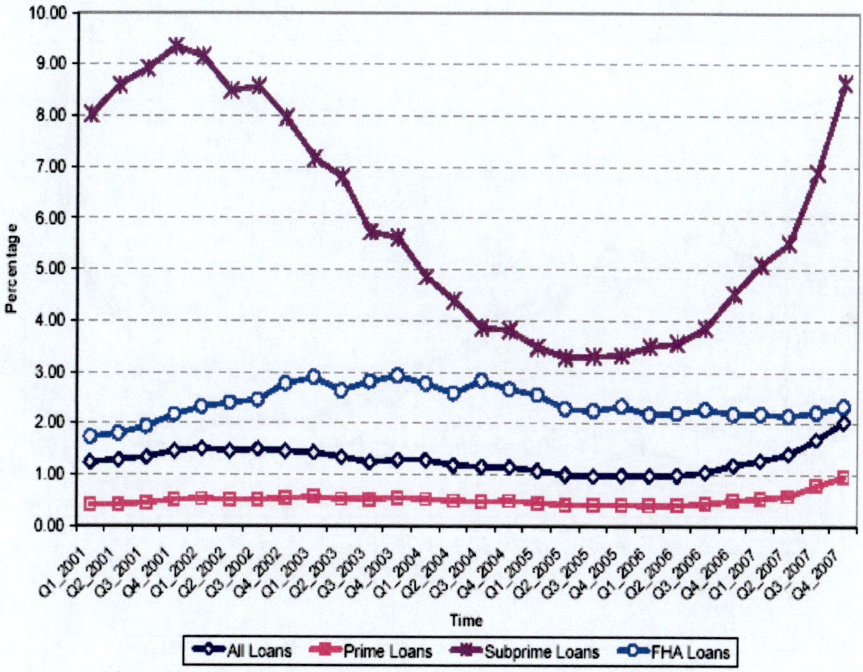

Source: Mortgage Bankers Association.

Figure 1. Percentage of Foreclosures by Aggregate Category.

Figure 1 indicates that subprime foreclosure rates have always been greater than prime and FHA foreclosure rates. When housing prices were rising and interest rates were falling between 2002 and 2005, the overall foreclosure rate for all loan categories was steady along with prime loans. Subprime foreclosure rates declined markedly between 2002 and 2005.[4] Foreclosures began to rise, however, in early 2006, and have continued rising through the fourth quarter of 2007. The average foreclosure rate for all subprime loans during this period was 5.20%, while the average foreclosure rate for all FHA loans was 2.22%. The foreclosure rate for all prime loans averaged 0.9 6%. Given a low prime foreclosure rate relative to the other loan type categories and the fact that prime loans make up a larger share of the mortgage market, the overall foreclosure rate for all loans in the survey averaged 1.33%. The maximum foreclosure rate over the entire period for all loans in the survey was 2.04%, which occurred during the fourth quarter of 2008. The rise in the overall foreclosure rate since 2006, therefore, reflects the large increase in subprime foreclosure rates.

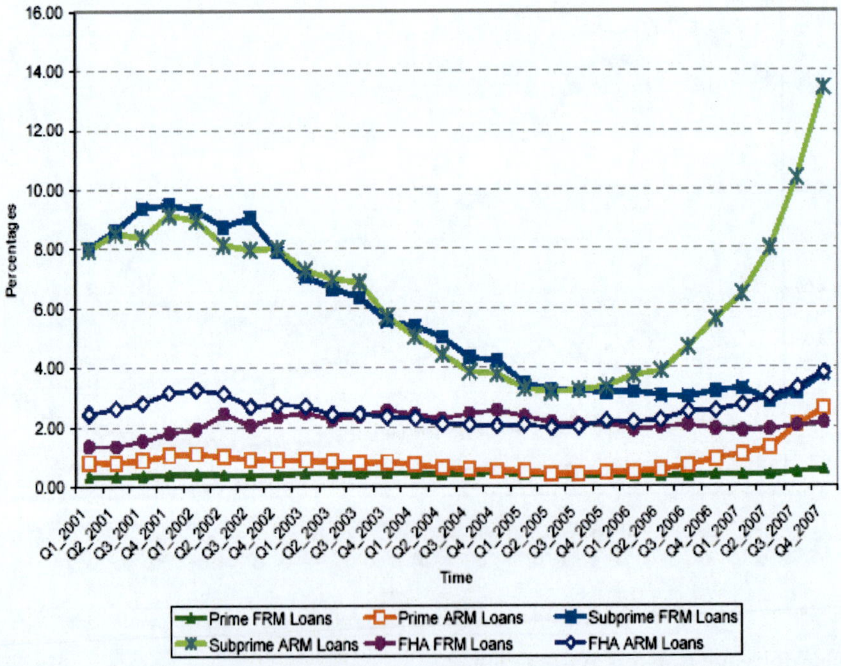

Source: Mortgage Bankers Association.

Figure 2. Percentage of Foreclosures FRM versus ARM.

In Figure 2, the composite categories have been further separated into fixed rate mortgage (FRM) foreclosures and adjustable rate mortgage (ARM) foreclosures. From 2006 to the fourth quarter of 2007, the subprime foreclosure rates are again the highest, followed by FHA, and then prime loans. The foreclosure rates averaged 3.18% for subprime FRM loans, 7.03% for subprime ARM loans, 1.97% for FHA FRM loans, 2.79% for FHA ARM loans, 0.41% for prime FRM loans, and 1.21% for prime ARM loans. The NDS does not report composite foreclosure rates for all FRM loans or all ARM loans. Based upon the information provided here, however, the overall FRM and ARM composite foreclosure rates are likely to be much lower than the equivalent rates computed for the subprime and FHA categories. Furthermore, the composite series of FRM loan foreclosure rates is likely to be lower than composite series of foreclosure rates for ARM loans.[5] The descriptive data in Figure 2 indicate that many of the foreclosures were associated with ARM loans, in particular, the subprime ARM loans.

If lenders effectively take into account information about creditworthiness (such as credit history, income, and wealth) when borrowers apply for loans, then foreclosures should reflect unpredictable changes in economic or personal circumstances that neither the borrower nor the lender can anticipate. Examples of unanticipated changes in personal circumstances include divorce, sudden changes in health, and job loss. Given no abnormal rise in national divorce rates or debilitating medical injuries, those reasons cannot fully explain the recent rise in foreclosures. Foreclosures could potentially be attributed to local unemployment conditions. For example, foreclosures in Ohio rose when its unemployment rate rose to approximately one percentage point higher than the annual U.S. national unemployment rate (5.5% compared with 4.6% in 2006). Rising job losses, however, still can not entirely account for aggregate developments. Florida, for instance, had unemployment rates at or below the U.S. national average during 2006, yet the state still experienced a marked rise in foreclosures. Hence, unanticipated changes in personal circumstances do not sufficiently explain the recent rise in foreclosures.

The slowdown in the rate of house price appreciation and sales activity are examples of unanticipated changes in economic circumstances that can potentially translate into a rise in foreclosures. According to the U.S. Census Bureau, new home prices between June 2006 and June 2007 fell by 4.11%, and new home sales were down by 22.18%. According to the National Association of Realtors, median existing home prices over the same period fell by 0.04%, and existing home sales declined by 11 .25%.[6] Falling house prices and the more rapid decline in home sales activity occurred simultaneously with the rise in foreclosure rates.

Borrowers with financial or cash flow problems are likely to find it difficult to avoid foreclosure when they cannot quickly sell their homes for prices that would cover most or all of their mortgage obligations. Refinancing or selling a home prior to an interest rate adjustment on an ARM loan, which may result in a substantial increase in the monthly payment, may not be feasible options in the current market. Houses may not appraise for amounts necessary to eliminate mortgage insurance premiums, which may have provided some reduction in the monthly payments for distressed borrowers. Given that more homes sit on the market for several months at a time, sellers are unable to raise listing prices to cover the outstanding mortgage, any owed property taxes, and any additional home equity loan expenses. The incentive for borrowers to default also increases when house values fall below the outstanding balance owed. Hence, a rise in foreclosures would not be considered unusual given the recent decline in housing market activity. Housing market activity and foreclosure rates are cyclical in nature, and typically move in opposite directions.

In addition to unanticipated housing market changes, the mortgage market also experienced structural changes, most notably, the expansion of the subprime market. Prior to this expansion, people with impaired credit were unable to obtain home equity or cash-out refinance loans from prime market lenders. Furthermore, when home prices began to exceed the maximum FHA loan limits in various regions, credit impaired borrowers looked for alternatives to FHA. Hence, the growth in subprime lending over the late 1990s and early to mid 2000s became the vehicle used to gain access to mortgage credit by people evaluated as having lesser credit quality. In fact, subprime loans are estimated to have accounted for 20% of all mortgage originations by 2005.[7] Given that the recent housing market slowdown is the first to include this structural change, it has become more apparent that subprime borrowers may be more susceptible to changing housing market conditions than prime borrowers, and perhaps those who satisfy current FHA requirements for mortgage insurance. Consequently, the perception of what should be considered a 'normal' rise in foreclosures rates during a housing market slowdown may arguably need to be revised upwards.

THE GENERAL FORECLOSURE PROCESS

Foreclosure is usually governed by state law, and the process varies widely by state. The description of the foreclosure process provided in this report, therefore, will be presented in very general terms. The process will be first explained assuming a traditional lending framework, followed by a brief explanation of how the process works when the mortgage has been securitized.

A Traditional Lending Framework

Foreclosure can begin after a borrower defaults on the mortgage loan.[8] Default is generally defined as being 90 days delinquent, although some lenders may use other definitions. Once in default, the lender must decide whether a loss mitigation or workout option would suffice, or whether to proceed with foreclosure, the process of recovering losses by repossessing and selling the property. A large incentive to resolve a default with an alternative loss mitigation option arguably exists because, as this report will show, foreclosure and subsequent disposition of the property can be a lengthy and costly process for the lender.[9] Homeowners with substantial equity in their home arguably have a greater incentive to cooperate with the lender and renegotiate an arrangement to avoid foreclosure. Foreclosures are, however, more likely to occur when homeowners have little (10% or less) equity in their homes. Moreover, if the value of a house falls below the value of the mortgage, or if very little or no downpayment was used to purchase the home, the borrower may have a financial incentive to walk away and not take the necessary steps to avoid foreclosure.[10]

The foreclosure processes can take anywhere from several months to almost two years depending upon the state. The lender must prove the borrower is in default, and follow various legal procedures prior to the authorization of a foreclosure auction to ensure a valid transfer of title. In *judicial foreclosure* states, a foreclosure petition must be heard and ruled upon by a judge who examines all of the evidence in the case. In the *power-of-sale* states, the lender holds a deed of trust with a clause that allows foreclosure without court action. Hence, it takes longer to complete foreclosure, and the associated costs are greater in judicial foreclosure states than in power-of-sale states, since more legal work is involved.

After proper notification requirements have been satisfied, the foreclosure auction begins. States typically require that the property owner be given some advance notice about when the foreclosure auction will take place. In addition, a legal advertisement must appear in local news media announcing the time and place of the auction, a legal description of the property, and the sale terms and conditions. At the auction, the auctioneer may begin with the reading of the legal advertisement and then set the minimum bid. The highest bidder at the conclusion of the bidding period assumes title and responsibility for the property.

Although the lender may prefer not to participate in the auction, which could result in assuming title to the property and additional carrying costs, there are legal and financial incentives for lenders to place a bid. First, the sale price of the foreclosed property should be at least 70% of the fair market value to prevent the former homeowner from successfully having the foreclosure overturned. If the property sold for an extremely low price, the difference between the current mortgage and the sale price, the remaining unpaid balance, is higher. Consequently, if the original mortgage was recourse debt, the former homeowner would be liable for a larger amount of debt. If the mortgage was nonrecourse debt, the unpaid mortgage debt is cancelled, and the borrower has received what is considered taxable income. The more debt discharged, the higher the tax liability.[11] The lending institution, therefore, could be accused of neglecting its fiduciary responsibility to the former homeowner to minimize the ensuing liability, especially if these liabilities were to result in insolvency. Under these circumstances, a lawsuit filed by the former homeowner against the lender could result in reversal of the foreclosure and perhaps an additional financial award for damages. Hence, the courts adopted a precedent after the *Durrett vs. Washington National Insurance Company* ruling in which a "reasonable" sale price on foreclosed property is approximately 70% of fair market value.[12] Lenders, therefore, may have to bid on the property to prevent the former homeowner from successfully having the foreclosure overturned.

Second, the lending institution has a financial incentive to minimize its losses. The lender may deem other bids to be too low and believe the property may fetch a higher market price depending upon current conditions. Of course, when house prices are rising, the lender may be able to recoup more losses than when they are declining, which means housing market conditions can be important. Because of these legal and financial incentives, the lender typically submits the highest bid at the foreclosure auction and winds up with the property title.

The foreclosure process does not necessarily end after title of the property is transferred. In nine states, the *statutory right of redemption* exists, which allows the borrower a period of time ranging from several months to a year to repurchase the property after the foreclosure auction. Regardless of whether the winning bid comes from the lender or some other auction participant, the foreclosure sale is not final in these states until the borrower has received a specified period of time to regain possession of the property. The homeowner regains possession by repaying the amount of the total indebtedness, which is determined by applicable state laws. Hence, the length of time from the initiation to completion of foreclosure process depends on whether the foreclosure must go to court and whether the right of redemption exists.

After incurring costs to foreclose, the lender incurs costs to sell the property purchased at auction. Given that the property is likely to be sold “AS IS” at auction, a foreclosed property may need rehabilitation before it can be used as a primary residence, an investment, or for resale. A foreclosed property acquired by a lender is accounted for as *real estate owned* (REO), which is the inventory of foreclosed houses lenders carry until resold. As with any seller, the lender may need to repair any deferred maintenance or outright damage in preparation to put the property on the market. Lenders still require the services of realty brokers, who are paid commissions, to sell REO properties. Meanwhile, the lender still incurs costs such as foregone interest, property taxes, and any other delinquent liabilities assumed from the previous borrower. Consequently, even if the property were sold at market value, the lender has incurred losses. The distinction of being a REO property, however, may have the effect of reducing the list price below current market value. Furthermore, the lender may pay some or all of closing costs to entice new buyers, just as any seller might do in any ordinary real estate transaction. Once title has been transferred to a new owner, the tabulation of the lender’s total foreclosure costs, from borrower default to final property disposition, may begin.

The discussion so far has focused upon a single lender foreclosing on a single mortgage. If the borrower used two loans to acquire the property, however, then two lenders would be affected. Suppose a borrower who has been foreclosed upon obtained a primary loan for 80% of the total loan amount and a ‘piggy-back’ or secondary loan for the remaining 20%. The proceeds of the REO sale generally go to pay off the primary lender first, who generally has priority, and the lender of the secondary loan gets whatever is left over. Given that foreclosure costs can be substantial, the second lender faces a greater possibility of not recouping anything on the unpaid secondary loan balance.

As stated earlier, lenders may initially want to try a loss mitigation solution with defaulted borrowers. Although a workout may result in a reduction of some of the expected revenues from the original mortgage agreement, the revenue loss may still be considered a far less costly alternative to foreclosure.[13] Of course, if a loan falls into default again after a loss mitigation option has previously been applied, the additional foregone interest expenses are also added to the overall foreclosure costs. Hence, loss mitigation may be a less costly alternative to foreclosure only if it is successful at ‘reperforming’ the mortgage loan, but substantially increases foreclosure costs if unsuccessful. For this reason, lenders may have mixed opinions and adopt different policies regarding the frequency of loss mitigation usage based upon their individual experiences.

Finally, it is important to note that foreclosures are rarely profitable for honest lenders. Fraudulent sellers profit by successfully selling overvalued properties. Damaged properties can be sold at inflated prices using fraudulent appraisals or making shoddy repairs that pass inspections. Should home buyers realize they may be victims of fraud and perhaps have loans higher than the actual property values, they may simply choose to walk away and allow the property to be foreclosed upon. The lender, who is likely to be saddled with an over-valued property that must be repaired and resold, may also be considered a victim of fraud under these circumstances.

A Structured Financing Framework

The term "lender" has previously been used under the more traditional context in which a bank that originates a mortgage holds it in portfolio. In modern financial markets, however, originators do not necessarily keep loans in their portfolios. Loans originated in the primary market, where the home purchaser and the loan originator conduct business, are often sold in the secondary market, where the loan originator and an investor conduct business. The process of structured financing in the mortgage market will be briefly explained in four steps.

First, a home buyer goes to an originator, which can be a financial institution or mortgage broker, who then approves and makes a mortgage loan. Second, the originator may then choose to sell the loan to a securitizer. A securitizer can be a government sponsored enterprise, such as Fannie Mae or Freddie Mac, or a private securitization trust.

Third, the securitizer has the responsibility of transforming the individual mortgages into asset- or mortgage-backed securities. These securities can be subdivided into various *tranches,* or groups of securities with specific risk and return characteristics. For example, suppose the securitizer decides to create a senior-junior tranching structure. The senior tranche may be designated as the one that gets paid out to its set of investors first, but the yield may be lower than the junior tranche, which is designated to be paid out last. When the securitizer decides to sell the tranches in the secondary market, the senior tranche will appeal to investors that prefer lower risk investments, and the junior tranche will appeal to investors that prefer to take higher risks for the possibility of earning a higher yield. The senior-junior tranching structure is only one of the numerous disbursement structures securitizers can use to entice investors. This particular tranching structure, however, is used throughout this report for the sake of illustration.

In the last step, the securitizer sells the tranches to investors, who become the ultimate "lenders." The investors are typically hedge funds, pension funds, or other financial institutions. (If the securitizer decides not to sell the securities to third party investors and hold them in its own portfolio, then the securitizer becomes the investor.) Investors generally have funds to invest and need securities with very specific risk or return characteristics. Financial institutions, in particular, hold assets and liabilities with revenue and payment streams that are often not synchronized, and asset-backed securities can be used to better match cash inflows and outflows. Hence, when securitizers can effectively identify and create securities that satisfy various investor needs in the secondary market, they can appeal to more investors and attract more credit, which can be used for the funding of loan originations in the primary market.

The key difference between the foreclosure process under a traditional banking versus a structured financing framework has to do with the amount of flexibility the mortgage holder has to make important financial decisions when default occurs. The degree of flexibility depends on whether the mortgage holder is the actual owner or an agent acting contractually on behalf of a set of owners. Suppose the securitizer either acts as or appoints a *servicer,* who collects mortgage payments from borrowers and disburse them to the tranches. The securitizer or investor is likely to establish rules that the servicer is contractually obligated to follow, since the servicer is an agent acting on behalf of the investor or securitizer. When default occurs, the rules have provisions that state: (1) whether or not the servicer can offer a loss mitigation solution, and if so, what types and limitations; (2) when the servicer can initiate foreclosure; (3) if the servicer may act as an agent at the foreclosure auction; and (4) any bidding rules the servicer must follow. For example, if a servicer has permission to initiate foreclosure, the rules are likely to state how much can be bid (e.g. up to a certain percentage or the full amount of a borrower's unpaid balance) at a foreclosure auction. Given that the costs associated with foreclosure will be borne by the ultimate investors, the rules are designed to minimize those expenses.[14]

Any foreclosure costs generated from defaulted mortgages in a pool of mortgage-backed securities must be subtracted from the proceeds paid to the securitization trust. Suppose the securitizer is currently using the senior-junior tranching structure described above. If the senior tranche gets paid first, then the junior tranche will initially suffer the revenue loss.[15] The investors in the senior tranche would be adversely affected should the number of foreclosures exceed expectations, and associated costs exceed the stream of revenues that would have been paid out to the junior tranche. Of course, fewer foreclosures can possibly translate into the junior tranche holders being rewarded with higher yield than senior holders, since they are compensated for assuming more default risk.[16]

Estimates of Foreclosure Costs

The legal fees, foregone interest, property taxes, repayment of delinquent obligations by the former homeowners, and selling expenses make foreclosures extremely costly to lenders.[17] Obtaining an estimate of foreclosure costs that can be attributed solely to the lender is difficult without proprietary data that is closely held by lenders and financial institutions. Many studies may provide a dollar value associated with foreclosure costs, but it is difficult to know how cost estimates were obtained without access to the proprietary data used in the studies.[18] A study cited in a Freddie Mac Working Paper estimated the total costs of foreclosure for a sample of loans was approximately $58,759 per loan.[19] Those costs include the interest lost during the delinquency period, foreclosure costs, and disposition of the property — costs that the lender would be likely to incur. The working paper does not state explicitly if these costs were paid by the lender, nor whether the $58,759 was an average or median amount per foreclosure, but it did say the foreclosure process took an average of 18 months to resolve. Hence, this reported dollar amount may be fairly representative of the actual costs incurred only by a single lender, presumably in 2002.[20]

Foreclosure costs are far-reaching. In addition to losing their homes, borrowers are likely to find it extremely difficult to obtain credit at low rates in the future, if they can even get loans. Lenders suffer the losses associated with acquiring the property from the borrower, settling outstanding claims, repairing any damages, and selling the property. Local governments may face the problem associated with vacant units in neighborhoods and loss of tax revenues. Foreclosure may reduce the value of neighboring homes. As a result, foreclosure is something that parties directly and indirectly involved with the property would want to avoid.[21]

COULD NATIONAL FORECLOSURE LAWS REDUCE COSTS?

For concerned or responsible parties considering a nationalized foreclosure process, an important question would be, would a more uniform process reduce costs? The answer depends upon whether the balance of rights in such a law favors the lender or the borrower. It may be argued that inconsistent and lengthy foreclosure periods create uncertainty, which drive up costs, and may possibly drive up lending costs for non-defaulting borrowers. Lenders may decide to charge higher rates and require higher downpayments, which could result in a reduction of the supply of credit, to defer anticipated losses.[22] Hence, reducing the time it takes for foreclosure shifts the balance of rights more toward the lender, which could reduce lender costs and perhaps costs to borrowers that do not have repayment problems.

On the other hand, a federal foreclosure law structured to favor borrowers would increase the time available for borrowers to avoid losing their homes. For example, a federal law could extend the statutory right of redemption to all states. If, however, federal laws did favor borrowers, it might be more difficult for borrowers to overturn foreclosures once they became final, since it would become increasingly difficult to argue that ample time was not provided to reach a resolution.

Finally, even if a federal foreclosure law were structured to represent a compromise, the impact on costs would be ambiguous. A process designed to take longer than a few months, but completed in less than two years, may result in costs increasing for lenders in states where the process moves rather quickly and declining for lenders in states where the process moves slowly. The net effect on a national cost estimate, therefore, is indeterminate. Under a federal foreclosure law, however, it may become easier to obtain a much more reliable national estimate of the actual foreclosure costs, since lenders would follow similar foreclosure procedures nationwide.

REFERENCES

[1] For more information about the Mortgage Bankers Association and the National Delinquency Survey, please go to [http://www.mbaa.org].

[2] For background and information about GSEs, CRS Report RS2 1724, *GSE Regulatory Reform: Frequently Asked Questions*, by N. Eric Weiss.

[3] See CRS Report RL33930, Subprime Mortgages: Primer on Current Lending and Foreclosure Issues, by Edward Vincent Murphy.

[4] FHA foreclosures saw an increase arguably because some of its more creditworthy borrower were refinancing out of FHA. These borrowers were either obtaining prime loans and no longer pay FHA mortgage insurance premiums or they wanted to obtain cash-out refinances that exceed the FHA loan limits, since house prices were rapidly appreciating. Hence, the rise in the FHA foreclosure rate might reflect a decrease in the denominator of total mortgage loans, rather than an increase in the numerator of total foreclosures.

[5] See CRS Report RL33775, Alternative Mortgages: Causes and Policy Implications of Troubled Mortgage Resets in the Subprime and Alt-A Markets, by Edward Vincent Murphy.

[6] The January 2006 to June 2007 time frame would have been chosen to coincide with the period the foreclosures began to rise as reported by the NDS. Some of the housing price and sales data, however, are not seasonally adjusted, making it necessary to use the June 2006 to June 2007 period for computing annual rates.

[7] See Robert B. Avery, Kenneth P. Brevoort, and Glenn B. Canner, "Higher-Priced Home Lending and the 2005 HMDA Data," *Federal Reserve Bulletin* (September 2008), p. A1 25.

[8] For a primer on delinquency, default, foreclosure, and loan workouts, see Charles A. Capone, "Research Into Mortgage Default and Affordable Housing: A Primer," prepared for the Local Initiatives Support Corporation for Home Ownership Summit 2001, November 8, 2001, http://www.lisc.org/files/906_file_asset_ upload_file755_ 793.pdf].

[9] Loss mitigation or 'workouts' refer to a menu of possible options to avoid foreclosure. Lenders may choose from various options, which may include rescheduling payments and restructuring loan, to help distressed borrowers become current and continue to stay current in payments. If borrower circumstances would not allow loans to reperform, agreement to a pre-foreclosure sell or deed-in-lieu of foreclosure may also be considered a form of loss mitigation.

[10] Although a borrower with little home equity may not suffer a major financial loss after foreclosure, the ability to obtain any subsequent loans may be severely affected for several years.

[11] The state where the mortgage is originated determines whether the mortgage is recourse or nonrecourse debt. For a discussion on recourse and nonrecourse debt as well as the tax liability issues associated with debt forgivness, see CRS Report RL342 12, *Analysis of the Proposed Tax*

Exclusion for Canceled Mortgage Debt Income, by Pamela J. Jackson and Erika Lunder.

[12] *Durrett v. Washington National Insurance Co.*, 621 F. 2d 201 (5th Cir. 1980). See Charles A. Capone, *Providing Alternatives to Mortgage Foreclosure: A Report to Congress,* Department of Housing and Urban Development, Washington, DC, 1996 at [http://www.huduser.org/Publications/pdf/alt.pdf] and Scott B. Ehrlich, "Avoidance of Foreclosure Sales as Fraudulent Conveyances: Accommodating Sate and Federal Objectives," *Virginia Law Review*, vol. 71, no. 6 (September 1985), pp. 933-980.

[13] The Federal Housing Administration (FHA) insures lenders against borrower default, and FHA, as opposed to the lender, initiates and disposes of foreclosed properties. Lenders that have FHA-insured mortgage loans in default, however, are required to show documentation that some form of loss mitigation was offered to borrowers. FHA will not incur the costs of foreclosure without first determining whether a loss mitigation option can be applied.

[14] See CRS Report RS22741, Is Securitization an Obstacle to Subprime Borrower Workouts?, by Edward Vincent Murphy.

[15] In some cases, securitizers may decide to keep a tranche in its portfolio, and the retained tranche would be referred to as *excess spread.* If a junior tranche were retained and became the excess spread, this tranche would consist of the cash flow remaining after the principle and yield to senior tranche holders, any loan servicing fees, and any losses associated with default and foreclosure costs were paid. The securitizer earns whatever cash remains, which provides a strong financial incentive to effectively minimize default and foreclosure costs. If the junior tranche is sold rather than retained in portfolio, the investors' payout would be the same, but the tranche would not be referred to as excess spread.

[16] The liquidity crisis of August 2007 was triggered by senior tranche holders reassessing the riskiness of their exposure to financial problems exceeding expectations. See CRS Report RL34 182, *Financial Crisis? The Liquidity Crunch of August 2007*, by Darryl E. Getter, Mark Jickling, Marc Labonte, and Edward Vincent Murphy.

[17] This section of the report returns to the generic use of the term 'lender', although the discussion is applicable to investors, who have servicers acting on their behalf.

[18] See Desiree Hatcher, *Foreclosure Alternatives: A Case for Preserving Homeownership,* Profitwise News and Views, published by the Federal Reserve Bank of Chicago (February 2006). The article mentions that GMAC-RFC (Residential Funding Corporation) reported losing $50,000 per foreclosed home.

[19] See Amy Crews Cutts and Richard K. Green, Innovative Servicing Technology: Smart Enough to Keep People in Their Houses?, Freddie Mac Working Paper #04-03 (July 2004). The authors cite Craig Focardi, Servicing Default Management: An Overview of the Process and Underlying Technology, TowerGroup Research Note, No. 033-1 3C (November 15, 2002). The $58,759 cited in the Freddie Mac report comes from Focardi's study.

[20] It is not clear whether the final sales price was subtracted from the gross costs in order to obtain the net cost of foreclosures to lenders. If this figure is net costs, then estimated foreclosure costs reflect current market conditions at the time the estimates were computed. Foreclosure costs are likely to be higher during 2006 and 2007 when housing market activity has slowed. Lenders would be unable to turn over foreclosed properties as quickly and market prices have declined in many areas over this period.

[21] The Joint Economic Committee estimates that foreclosures on average may cost as much as $80,000. This estimate includes costs to homeowners, loan servicers, lenders, neighbors, and local governments. See U.S. Congress, Senate Joint Economic Committee, *Sheltering Neighborhoods from the Subprime Foreclosure Storm*, Report by Joint Economic Committee, 110th 1st sess. (Washington: GPO 2007) [http://jec.senate.gov/Documents/Reports/subprime 11 apr2007 Rev. pdf]

[22] See Karen M. Pence, "Foreclosing on Opportunity: State Laws and Mortgage Credit," *Review of Economics and Statistics*, vol. 88, no. 1 (2006), pp.177-182. This study finds average loan sizes smaller in states with more protections for borrowers, which could translate into higher costs on all borrowers in those states.

In: Understanding Mortgage Meltdowns
Editor: A. V. Carey

ISBN: 978-1-60692-789-2

Chapter 5

CONSTITUTIONAL ISSUES RELATING TO PROPOSALS FOR LEGISLATION TO IMPOSE AN INTEREST RATE FREEZE/REDUCTION ON EXISTING MORTGAGES*

David H. Carpenter

ABSTRACT

The U.S. housing market began to slow in early 2006. This downturn has likely played a role in the rise of late mortgage payments and foreclosures occurring across the country over the past year. Many believe that the problem will get worse. The Joint Economic Committee estimates that around 2 million foreclosures of subprime mortgages will occur from the beginning of 2007 to the end of 2009.

As a way to slow the decline, some in Congress have suggested passing legislation that would impose a temporary reduction or freeze in the interest rates of certain mortgages in order to give mortgage market participants, such as borrowers, servicers, lenders, and investors, time to refinance, or otherwise adjust the mortgage terms of borrowers who would not likely be able to keep up with their scheduled payments. Such a measure would modify existing contracts, which would result in the loss of property rights of some

---

* This is an edited, excerpted and augmented edition of a Congressional Research Service Publication RL34379, dated June 11, 2008.

individuals in the mortgage market. For this reason, this type of legislation raises some constitutional issues.

This report addresses the possible constitutional implications, most notably regarding the Fifth Amendment's Takings Clause, of a temporary interest rate freeze/reduction as it would relate to investors in mortgage-backed securities (MBSs), which may aid the crafting of such proposals. This report does not seek to address a specific legislative proposal; rather, it merely analyzes interest rate freezes/reductions, generally. MBS investors are chosen for analysis in this report because they likely would be impacted more by such a measure than other potential claimants. However, this is not to suggest that other mortgage market participants could not or would not raise legal challenges because of an interest rate freeze/reduction.

This report presents an overview of Congress's authority, pursuant to the Commerce and Bankruptcy Clauses, to pass laws pertaining to mortgages, and reviews Contract Clause, Substantive Due Process, and Takings Clause jurisprudence. After explaining why Contract Clause and Substantive Due Process claims appear less relevant to the question, this report considers the test a court would likely use in assessing whether a federal interest rate freeze/reduction would offend the Takings Clause, while pointing out that courts could apply a different test in this situation. It also suggests that courts' analyses could vary according to whether they focus on the impact that an interest rate freeze/reduction has on whole MBS trusts or specific investment tranches of those trusts. Where the focus is on tranches of mortgage-backed securitized trusts, a federal interest rate freeze/reduction, in a minority of cases, potentially could be considered a "taking" requiring just compensation for the purpose of the Fifth Amendment. Such a finding would be even less likely where the focus is on the impact to whole trusts. The number of likely successful claims and the overall potential liability of the federal government for those claims (and the litigation costs of unsuccessful claims) is not possible to assess, at least within the scope of this report.

INTRODUCTION AND BACKGROUND

The U.S. housing market began to slow in early 2006. This downturn has likely played a role in the rise of late mortgage payments and foreclosures occurring across the country over the past year.[1] Many believe that the problem will get worse. The Joint Economic Committee estimates that around 2 million foreclosures of subprime mortgages will occur from the beginning of 2007 to the end of 2009.[2]

As a way to slow the decline, some in Congress have suggested passing legislation that would impose a temporary reduction or freeze in the interest rates of certain mortgages in order to give mortgage market participants, such as borrowers, servicers, lenders, and investors, time to refinance, or otherwise adjust the mortgage terms of borrowers who would not likely be able to keep up with their scheduled payments. Such a measure would modify existing contracts, which would result in the loss of property rights of some individuals in the mortgage market. For this reason, this type of legislation raises some constitutional issues.

This report addresses the possible constitutional implications, most notably regarding the Fifth Amendment's Takings Clause, of a temporary interest rate freeze/reduction as it would relate to investors in mortgage-backed securities (MBSs), which may aid the crafting of such proposals. This report does not seek to address a specific legislative proposal; rather, it merely analyzes interest rate freezes/reductions, generally. MBS investors are chosen for analysis in this report because they likely would be impacted more by such a measure than other potential claimants. However, this is not to suggest that other mortgage market participants could not or would not raise legal challenges because of an interest rate freeze/reduction.

This report presents an overview of Congress's authority, pursuant to the Commerce and Bankruptcy Clauses, to pass laws pertaining to mortgages, and reviews Contract Clause, Substantive Due Process, and Takings Clause jurisprudence. After explaining why Contract Clause and Substantive Due Process claims appear less relevant to the question, this report considers the test a court would likely use in assessing whether a federal interest rate freeze/reduction would offend the Takings Clause, while pointing out that courts could apply a different test in this situation. It also suggests that courts' analyses could vary according to whether they focus on the impact that an interest rate freeze/reduction has on whole MBS trusts or specific investment tranches of those trusts. Where the focus is on tranches of mortgage-backed securitized trusts, a federal interest rate freeze/reduction, in a minority of cases, potentially could be considered a "taking" requiring just compensation for the purpose of the Fifth Amendment. Such a finding would be even less likely where the focus is on the impact to whole trusts. The number of likely successful claims and the overall potential liability of the federal government for those claims (and the litigation costs of unsuccessful claims) is not possible to assess, at least within the scope of this report.[3]

LEGISLATIVE AUTHORITY TO PASS AN INTEREST RATE FREEZE/REDUCTION

The constitutionality of legislation that imposes an interest rate freeze/reduction on mortgages may be affected by the context in which it is raised, and by extension the authority by which Congress passes such a statute. For example, a piece of legislation providing general, regulatory reform of the housing finance market is more likely to fall under Congress's Commerce Clause authority. Whereas, legislation that is more tailored to asset allocation between a debtor and her creditors is more likely to be considered an extension of Congress's Bankruptcy Clause authority. The parameters of Congress's authority pursuant to these two clauses are addressed in turn.

The Constitution grants Congress vast authority to enact laws involving interstate commerce. Article I, § 8, clause 3 of the U.S. Constitution states: "Congress shall have the Power To ... regulate Commerce with foreign Nations and among the several States ...." Commerce "among the several States" must, by "necessity" include commerce "between the states."[4] The power extends beyond the borders of individual states because it would not be possible for Congress to regulate commerce that takes place exclusively on states' borders.

While there was a time when the courts interpreted the Commerce Clause more restrictively, the melding of 50 different economies into a single national economy has played a significant role in its expansion.[5] Indeed, the U.S. Supreme Court has only twice since the 1930s invalidated federal legislation because Congress had exceeded its Commerce Clause power. In both of those cases, the Court held that the statute being challenged was not economic in nature, and therefore, did not have a substantial effect on interstate commerce.[6]

The Court has said that statutes that regulate one of three categories of commercial activities are within congressional authority:

> First, Congress may regulate the use of the channels of interstate commerce. Second, Congress is empowered to regulate and protect the instrumentalities of interstate commerce, or persons or things in interstate commerce, even though the threat may come only from intrastate activities. Finally, Congress' commerce authority includes the power to regulate those activities having a substantial relation to interstate commerce, i.e., those activities that substantially affect interstate commerce.[7]

The last of these categories allows courts to examine the cumulative effect of a commercial activity on the economy as a whole. This is the category within which an interest rate freeze/reduction likely would fall.

A federally mandated interest rate freeze/reduction designed to reduce the effects of a slowing national housing market seems to pertain to financial transactions that, "viewed in the aggregate, substantially affect interstate commerce."[8] Even if viewed as entirely intrastate, such a law also would likely be considered "part of a larger regulation of economic activity, in which the regulatory scheme could be undercut unless the intrastate activity were regulated," due to the fact that the secondary market links local real property into a national market.[9] Although not beyond debate, it seems likely that a court would find a statute imposing an interest rate freeze/reduction to be within Congress's constitutional authority.

Congress also has broad authority, concurrent with its authority under the Commerce Clause, to enact "uniform laws on the subject of Bankruptcies."[10] The Supreme Court has approved of Congress's use of this authority to impair contracts and even to avoid liens.[11] In fact, the modification of contract rights is one of the main purposes of bankruptcy. For these reasons, if a court finds such legislation to be a valid extension of Congress's bankruptcy power, then that court may provide Congress greater deference under a takings analysis than it would for legislation passed pursuant to the Commerce Clause.[12]

Whether or not an interest rate freeze/reduction would fall within the Bankruptcy Clause likely would depend on the scope and nature of a specific proposal, as well as Congress's intent for its passage. The more limited the application of such legislation is to debtors who meet the qualifications to file for bankruptcy, probably the more likely a court would find the legislation to be a valid extension of bankruptcy power. Such a determination also may be contingent upon a court's interpretation of the breadth of Congress's power under the Bankruptcy Clause, which cannot be predicted.[13]

Regardless of which of these two sources of authority are applied, the legislative proposal in question would still be subject to certain constitutional protections such as those provided by the Fifth Amendment's Due Process and Takings Clauses.

Contract Clause and Substantive due Process

Before discussing the relevant portions of the Fifth Amendment, some common misconceptions regarding the Contract Clause should be addressed. Article I, § 10, clause 1 of the U.S. Constitution states: "No State shall ... pass any ... Law impairing the Obligation of Contracts...." This clause prohibits states from passing legislation that makes certain changes to the terms of existing contracts.[14] The language of the Contract Clause is expressly limited to the states. Additionally, the Court has held that the principles of the Contract Clause are not incorporated against the federal government by the Fifth Amendment's Due Process Cause.[15] The Court explained:

> We have never held ... that the principles embodied in the Fifth Amendment's Due Process Clause are coextensive with provisions existing against state impairments of pre-existing contracts.... [Rather,] we have contrasted the limitations imposed on States by the Contract Clause with the less searching standards imposed on economic legislation by the Due Process Clauses.[16]

Therefore, the Contract Clause does not apply to federal legislation.

Federal legislation, on the other hand, is subject to the protections of substantive due process. Substantive due process "prevents government power from being used for purposes of oppression, or abuse of government power that shocks the conscience, or action that is legally irrational in that it is not sufficiently keyed to any legitimate government purpose."[17] An interest rate freeze/reduction that is implemented for the purpose of providing lenders and servicers time to initiate loan modifications and loss mitigation in order to strengthen an ailing market would not likely be violative of substantive due process in light of the vast deference courts provide the government in the context of economic regulation.[18] Consequently, this report focuses on takings law analysis.[19]

OVERVIEW OF TAKINGS CLAUSE JURISPRUDENCE

The Fifth Amendment concludes with the words "nor shall private property be taken for public use, without just compensation." The Takings Clause requires striking a balance between the government's public goals and the burdens suffered by private property owners as the government takes measures to meet its goals. The courts have recognized relatively few governmental infringements of private citizens' property as constitutional "takings" where no outright seizure or permanent physical occupation of the property occurs. The infringement must rise to a certain severity or be of a particular kind before courts will say a "taking" has occurred.

Only then must the government provide "just compensation" to the property owner.[20] The courts have developed an array of tests, rules, and factors to determine what does and does not constitute a "taking."

Four Types of Takings

The proper test to apply depends on the type of governmental action involved. There are four broad categories of takings recognized by the Supreme Court.[21] Two of these tests are clearly not applicable to an interest rate freeze/reduction. One is a land-use exaction taking, such as a mandatory set aside for a certain portion of a new housing development to be green space.[22] The other is a type of regulatory taking, as described in *Lucas v. South Carolina Coastal Council*,[23] where the government "deprive[s] an owner of all economically beneficial use of her property." This type of infringement is considered a per se taking and is commonly referred to as a *Lucas* "total taking."[24] Most courts agree that *Lucas* total takings only apply to land, not personal property such as contract rights.[25] An interest rate freeze/reduction could be assessed pursuant to one of the other two tests. One is a "physical taking" or "appropriation" where the "government requires an owner to suffer permanent physical invasion of her property."[26] The final test is for all regulatory takings other than total takings, which are analyzed pursuant to the test originally set out in *Penn Central Transp. Co. v. City of New York*.[27]

Physical Taking/Appropriation vs. Regulatory Taking

Plaintiffs would likely argue that legislation imposing an interest rate freeze/reduction resulted in a "permanent physical occupation" of their property, as these are considered per se takings, warranting just compensation. While on the contrary, the government would likely argue that this type of legislation should be analyzed under *Penn Central*, where the government usually wins. One takings law commentator explains:

> The Court's decisions using per se physical taking analysis ... typically involve physical invasions in the literal sense — invasions by aircraft, flood waters, the boating public, government personnel, cable

> boxes, and mobile-home-park tenants. But in some factual contexts ... physical and regulatory takings have proved difficult to keep separate.
>
> The tendency to blur the two is enhanced by the powerful incentives plaintiffs have to urge a physical, versus regulatory, theory in a case. First, there is the lesser showing needed for plaintiff to win on a permanent physical occupation claim.... Second, ... [is] the extremely narrow range of application for the ... total taking test, leaving the physical occupation rule as the only per se rule left to plaintiff in many cases.... [One example of where this line is blurred is where a] government program causes no physical invasion, but affects the property owner in a way more or less akin to an appropriation. Here, the takings analysis may go either way — regulatory or physical. The issue played out at length in cases involving state demands that small interest amounts on lawyers' trust accounts be paid to a state-run program funding legal services for the poor, and was ultimately resolved as a physical-type taking.[28]

It is possible that a court would consider an interest rate freeze/reduction a physical taking or an appropriation of an MBS investor's rights to the income stream lost due to the legislation, and therefore, a per se taking. This argument would likely be given some credence because the focus of the proposals being considered for legislation, interest payments, is such a central element of a mortgage. What might be fundamental to a court's inquiry is whether the interest rate modification would have been allowed under the Pooling and Servicing Agreement (PSA). PSAs are the contracts for mortgage-backed securitized trusts that govern the legal relationship between MBS trustees, MBS investors, and servicers of the mortgages comprising these trusts. While not all PSAs are exactly alike, one relevant feature of typical agreements is the scope of the permission of servicers to perform loss mitigation and loan modification for borrowers. In instances where a mortgage would qualify for an interest rate freeze/reduction under federal legislation, but where the borrower would not have qualified for a modification under the PSA, finding a physical taking would be more likely. The more tailored the scope of any legislation to the situations in which servicers have authority to adjust mortgage interest rates pursuant to governing PSAs, the less likely a court would find a physical taking.[29]

A more probable scenario, especially in light of the fact that the income lost as a result of an interest rate freeze/reduction would not directly accrue to the government, as was the case with the interest from the lawyer's trust accounts, is that a court would consider such a statute as a possible regulatory taking, to be analyzed pursuant to *Penn Central*.

Historical Precedent: *Vinton Branch* and *Radford*

While it seems most likely in light of recent jurisprudence that courts would address a takings claim raised in response to an interest rate freeze/reduction under the parameters set out in *Penn Central*, it is possible that a court might be influenced by the similar fact patterns of two Supreme Court cases from the 1930s, *Wright v. Vinton Branch[30]* and *Louisville Joint Stock Land Bank v. Radford*.[31]

Congress enacted the Frazier-Lemke Act of 1934, which amended the Bankruptcy Act to provide farmers a five-year mortgage foreclosure moratorium, allow farmers to keep possession of real property for a reasonable rent, and allow them to pay a judicially appraised purchase value at the end of the five years for the purpose of preventing widespread farm foreclosures.[32] The Supreme Court in *Radford* held the Frazier-Lemke Act to be in violation of the Fifth Amendment, and thus unconstitutional.[33] The Court stated:

> The decision in the Radford case did not question the power of Congress to offer to distressed farmers the aid of a means of rehabilitation under the bankruptcy clause [sic]. The original Frazier-Lemke Act was there held invalid solely on the ground that the bankruptcy power of Congress, like its other great powers, is subject to the Fifth Amendment; and that, as applied to the mortgages given before its enactment, the statute violated that Amendment, since it effected a substantial impairment of the mortgagee's security. The opinion enumerates five important substantive rights in specific property which had been taken. It was not held that the deprivation of any one of these rights would have rendered the Act invalid, but that the effect of the statute in its entirety was to deprive the mortgagee of his property without due process of law. The rights enumerated were:
>
> 1 The right to retain the lien until the indebtedness thereby secured is paid.
> 2 The right to realize upon the security by a judicial public sale.
> 3 The right to determine when such sale shall be held, subject only to the discretion of the court.
> 4 The right to protect its interest in the property by bidding at such sale whenever held, and thus to assure having the mortgaged property devoted primarily to the satisfaction of the debt, either through receipt of the proceeds of a fair competitive sale or by taking the property itself.

5 The right to control meanwhile the property during the period of default, subject only to the discretion of the court, and to have the rents and profits collected by a receiver for the satisfaction of the debt.[34]

However, the *Radford* decision was called into question just three years later by the *Vinton Branch* Court, in which a slightly modified version of the Frazier-Lemke Act, which was found to no longer deprive three of the five above-listed substantive rights, was deemed in accordance with the Fifth Amendment.[35] The Court explained:

> The power here exerted by Congress is the broad power "To establish ... uniform Laws on the subject of Bankruptcies throughout the United States." The question which the objections raise is not whether the Act does more than modify remedial rights. It is whether the legislation modifies the secured creditor's rights, remedial or substantive, to such an extent as to deny the due process of law guaranteed by the Fifth Amendment.... For the reasons stated, we are of opinion that the provisions of subsection (s) [of the Frazier-Lemke Act] make no unreasonable modification of the mortgagee's rights; and hence are valid.[36]

While it is possible that a current court would look to *Vinton Branch* as authoritative on the question of a takings claim raised as a result of a federal interest rate freeze/reduction because that opinion addresses similar facts as those assessed in this report and because it has not been expressly overruled, it seems more likely that a court would analyze such a takings claim under the test outlined in *Penn Central.*

First of all, the *Vinton Branch* decision came down more than 40 years prior to *Penn Central.* In those 40 years and the subsequent 30, much has changed in takings jurisprudence.[37] Most notably, *Vinton Branch* was delivered at a time in which the courts did not delineate between the Fifth Amendment's Due Process Clause and the Fifth Amendment's Takings Clause. This point is emphasized by the varying language used in the *Radford* and *Vinton Branch* cases. The *Radford* decision states that the ultimate question to be addressed is "whether the Frazier-Lemke Act as applied has *taken from the Bank without compensation*, and given to Radford, rights in specific property which are of substantial value."[38] Whereas the *Vinton Branch* opinion characterizes the ultimate question as whether the act "modifies the secured creditor's rights ... to such an extent as to *deny the due process of law* guaranteed by the Fifth Amendment."[39] It was not until the 2005 Supreme Court decision, *Lingle v. Chevron U.S.A. Inc.*, that the High Court made it clear that the tests to be applied under takings claims are distinct from those analyzing potential due process violations.[40] The *Lingle* Court confirmed that:

> a plaintiff seeking to challenge a government regulation as an uncompensated taking of private property may proceed under one of the other theories discussed above — by alleging a "physical" taking, a *Lucas*-type "total regulatory taking," a *Penn Central* taking, or a land-use exaction violating the standards set forth in *Nollan* and *Dolan*.[41]

While *Penn Central* is likely to govern, this does not mean that a piece of legislation crafted to meet the test set out in *Vinton Branch* could not also pass the three balancing factors of *Penn Central*. These three factors are analyzed in great detail below, but as an example, an interest rate freeze/reduction statute that lasts for a relatively short period of time and that requires borrowers to make reasonable monthly payments in order to qualify for the interest rate adjustment will reduce the economic impact of the legislation on MBSs (mortgage-backed securities) investors' property rights, thus diminishing the strength of their takings arguments.

Application of *Penn Central* to an Interest Rate Freeze/Reduction

Penn Central Overview

Before beginning any analysis, it should be noted that Takings Clause jurisprudence is a highly amorphous and an ever-evolving area of the law. Additionally, the question of whether a statutorily imposed interest rate freeze/reduction violated the Takings Clause has never been addressed directly by a court. The *Penn Central* test is, as the Supreme Court has stated, an "essentially ad hoc and factual inquir[y]."[42] Finally, the mortgage-backed securities industry is a highly complex, yet largely unregulated industry, which makes garnering specific information about the tranches of each mortgage-backed securitized trust very difficult. All of these factors make analysis of how a court might rule on a takings issue quite difficult even where all facts are known. With those caveats in mind, the following analysis informs on how courts have assessed each of the three *Penn Central* factors and highlights certain contexts or facts that courts emphasize as triggering Takings Clause protection that may be implicated by such legislation.

Legislation targeting private contracts usually survives takings attacks under *Penn Central* analysis.[43] However, this does not mean that a court could not find a takings under certain circumstances, nor does it mean that secondary market investors would not bring suits claiming takings had occurred, which comes with its own costs to the government. It seems plausible, as discussed in greater detail below, that a statute imposing an interest rate freeze/reduction could have a significant enough effect on a minority of MBS tranches as to rise to the level of a taking.

The *Penn Central* test consists of three factors that are designed to determine whether the government regulatory action has resulted in the deprivation of a property right sufficient to violate the Takings Clause. The three factors are: (1) the economic impact of the government action; (2) the "extent to which the regulation has interfered with distinct investment-backed expectations"; and (3) the character of the government action.[44] The Supreme Court has shed little light on the content of these three factors or on how to balance them, and each factor raises "vexing subsidiary questions."[45]

Economic Impact

The *Penn Central* inquiry "turns in large part, albeit not exclusively" on the economic impact factor.[46] In assessing the economic impact, courts evaluate the proportion of the loss caused by the regulation to the "parcel as a whole."[47] This means that, in weighing the economic impact, the courts look at entire property, rather than exclusively at the portion of the real property affected by the legislation in isolation. The Supreme Court explained it this way:

> a claimant's parcel of property could not first be divided into what was taken and what was left for the purpose of demonstrating the taking of the former to be complete and hence compensable. To the extent that any portion of property is taken, that portion is always taken in its entirety; the relevant question, however, is whether the property taken is all, or only a portion of, the parcel in question.[48]

The "parcel as a whole" concept has three different dimensions: physical/spatial, functional, and temporal. In the context of a takings claim raised by investors of MBSs, compelling arguments could be made to define the physical "parcel" as either the tranches of each trust or the securitized trust as a whole. This report focuses on the tranches as the physical parcel interpretation because such a definition would result in the strongest arguments for a taking, thus emphasizing potential legal issues that interest rate freeze/reduction legislation may raise, which is the purpose of this report. The other option would make a successful takings claim less likely because the impact of such an interest rate change would be spread out over the hundreds or thousands of other mortgages within each trust.

To address the functional dimension, courts would look to how the governmental interference affects the entire "bundle of rights," as opposed to a single right within the bundle.[49] In the MBS context, an investor's bundle of rights would include everything provided in the governing PSA, including rights to a certain income stream and contract claims for violations of the PSA. The temporal dimension requires an assessment of the physical parcel for the entire time period during which the plaintiff has an interest in that property.[50] For example, if an investor owned a tranche that consisted of the 12-month income stream, from both principal and interest payments, of a group of mortgages, and a six-month interest rate freeze was imposed in the middle of that period, the court would analyze the economic impact to that investor in relation to the whole 12 months, not just the six months of the freeze (temporal dimension) and in relation to the income from both principal and interest, not just the interest payments changed by the freeze (functional).

Courts vary in how they determine the economic loss caused by regulations. Most courts look to either the property's "diminution in value" or "diminution in return" caused by the regulation.[51] Under both, courts are in agreement that the loss must be significant. The Supreme Court has in past cases found diminutions in property upwards of 75% to not, by themselves, be enough to be considered a "taking."[52] Determining the severity of the lost value or return caused by the legislation in question would be an entirely fact-specific inquiry.

The complexity of the secondary market coupled with its lack of governmental oversight, hamper the ability to fully assess how many, and to what extent, tranches of mortgage-backed securitized trusts would be affected by a statutorily imposed interest rate freeze/reduction of certain mortgages. When mortgages are sold in the secondary market, they are often lumped in trust and then separated into tranches on the basis of certain common characteristics. Mortgages can be left intact or they can be diced into pieces. For example, a tranche could consist entirely of 30-year, fixed, prime rate mortgages that do not include prepayment penalties. Or, a tranche could consist of only the income stream from the interest payments of subprime mortgages with two-year ARMs. Or, a tranche could be comprised of 25% of the first group and 75% of the second group. There are virtually no limits to what can comprise a tranche.

It is conceivable that there are or would be tranches that represent, in whole or in part, the income from the planned interest rate adjustment that is eliminated or significantly reduced by a federal interest rate freeze or reduction. In these cases, legislation could result in up to a 100% diminution in value or diminution in return of the tranches. Where a tranche loses its entire value due to federal legislation, a taking likely has occurred. It is unclear where a court would draw the line in cases where some, but less than a 100% loss results, though almost certainly, the percentage would be quite high. For intermediate percentages, the other two prongs of the *Penn Central* test likely are to be of importance.

Impairment of Investment-Backed Expectations

When .examining whether congressional impairment of private contracts interferes with investment- backed expectations, courts typically have focused on whether it was reasonable for the harmed party to assume that the impairment would not occur.[53] "The critical question is whether extension of existing law could be foreseen as reasonably possible."[54] To do so, courts generally look to the type and level of regulation the claimant faced prior to implementation of the regulation in question. If, for instance, the subject of the regulation was part of a "heavily regulated field" prior to the additional legislative impairment, then additional regulation is more likely to have been "foreseeable" to the harmed party. The courts have concluded, for example, that national banks[55] and employee pension plans[56] are in heavily regulated fields.[57] However, low-income housing is not.[58]

The proposals for legislation addressed in this report would regulate the mortgage lending, mortgage servicing, and mortgage-backed securities investing industries. The mortgage lending industry would likely be considered "heavily regulated." However, credible arguments could be made that the other two, especially, the MBSs industry, are not heavily regulated, which would strengthen the argument that a taking has occurred. Yet, secondary market investors understand that each mortgage they invest in could end up in default, and this possibility is accounted for in the PSAs governing when and how servicers may modify these loans. While a government imposed modification of the interest rates of certain mortgages arguably would be a departure from the norm of servicers modifying mortgages in accordance with the terms of PSAs, the more important question would seem to be whether the statutorily imposed modification would have been allowed pursuant to the governing PSA.

A MBS investor could make a stronger argument that the legislation in question was not reasonably foreseeable where the statutorily imposed interest rate freeze/reduction would not have been allowed under the governing PSA. The more tailored the application of any interest rate freeze/reduction was to those borrowers who would qualify for such a loan modification pursuant to the governing PSA, the fewer MBS investors that would have stronger arguments under this prong. Consequently, the scope of legislation might play an important role in a court's analysis under the investment-backed expectations prong of the *Penn Central* test.

Another factor that may strengthen a foreseeability argument, and thus augment the government's defense against a takings claim, is if the legislation in question is considered to be a valid extension of Congress's authority to pass laws on bankruptcies. Because the modification of contract rights is such an integral part of bankruptcy and because MBS investors should be aware that all mortgages could end up in bankruptcy, these investors arguably should be less surprised by a change to the bankruptcy laws that impose some form of interest rate freeze or reduction, than a more broadly applicable statute passed pursuant to the Commerce Clause.[59]

Character of the Government Action

The third factor, the character of the government action, is arguably of diminished importance in light of the Supreme Court's *Lingle v. Chevron USA Inc.* decision, where the Court stated unequivocally that inquiry into whether a regulation advances some public purpose is not relevant to the question of whether a taking occurred for Fifth Amendment purposes.[60] The effect *Lingle* will have on how future courts will apply the "nature of the government action" factor is presently unclear. Historically, courts used this factor to assess whether a regulation that impaired private contracts directly benefited the government; disproportionately imposed the costs of a public benefit on a small class; or was somehow the result of governmental bad faith.[61] It is doubtful that a legislatively imposed interest rate freeze/reduction would take rights from investors and appropriate them to the government or would be enacted as a result of bad faith. Rather, such legislation likely would be an attempt to help stem the current housing downturn that is affecting the entire market. In the absence of specific legislative language to delineate which mortgages would be covered by an interest rate freeze/reduction, it is unclear if such legislation would impose a disproportionate amount of liability on a small number of investors. The nature of the government action authorized by the proposals in question would not appear to greatly augment a takings claim, but more information would be needed to know for sure.

CONCLUSION

In sum, it is unlikely, but possible that a court would assess an interest rate freeze/reduction pursuant to the test outlined in the 1937 Supreme Court decision, *Vinton Branch.* Courts would be more likely to assess such legislation as a regulatory taking under *Penn Central*. If analyzed as a regulatory taking, it is unclear how a court would decide an as-applied takings claim, especially without specific facts that would allow an assessment of the severity of the regulation's economic impact on an individual investor's property rights, which seems to be the most important *Penn Central* factor.[62] In such an analysis, a court could define the physical parcel as either the securitized trust in its entirety or the investment tranches of each trust. If a court adopts the tranche as the parcel interpretation, it is not difficult to envision some tranches being significantly, if not entirely, diminished in value by an interest rate freeze/reduction, due to the great diversity of investments in the mortgage securities market. The economic impact in some of these situations could be substantial enough to be considered a regulatory taking. Finding a taking would be far less likely if a court accepts the argument that the physical parcel should be defined as an entire trust.

It is impossible to predict at what level of economic impact a court would hold that a taking has occurred, though in the past, it has almost always been quite high. The strength of an impairment of investment-backed expectations argument would likely turn on the scope of the legislation and how that coincides with the loan modification authority provided by the governing PSA and if a court determines the legislation to be passed pursuant to Congress's bankruptcy powers. The nature of the government action does not appear to warrant takings concerns on its own.

If a taking were found, then the legislation would stand, but the government would be required to provide claimants just compensation for their losses. There is no way to predict how much, if any, the government would be liable for in just compensation claims, but in an industry valued at more than $1 trillion in 2006, the potential liability could be large.[63] Additionally, investors who lost large sums of money due to an interest rate freeze/reduction could sue the government, and regardless of the outcome of these cases, the litigation itself would likely be costly.

REFERENCES

[1] See CRS Report RL33930, Subprime Mortgages: Primer on Current Lending and Foreclosure Issues, by Edward Vincent Murphy, and CRS Report RS225 11, Preliminary Observations on the Impact of the Bankruptcy Abuse Prevention and Consumer Protection Act of 2005 (P.L. 109-8), by Brian Cashell, Mark Jickling, and Heather D. Negley. See also, Joint Economic Committee, "Mortgage Woes Weigh on Financial Markets," September 11, 2007, available at [http://www.house.gov/jec/Economic%20Update/RED%20September%20 11 .pdf].

[2] Joint Economic Committee, "The Subprime Lending Crisis: The Economic Impact on Wealth, Property Values and Tax Revenues, and How We Got Here," October 2007, available at [http://jec.senate.gov/Documents/Reports/1 0.25 .07OctoberSubprimeReport. pdf].

[3] Quantifying the potential liability would require details of all, or a representative subsection of, the tranches of mortgage-backed securitized trusts. Because investors of these securities are largely unregulated, this information may not exist at all. If it does exist, the information is likely proprietary.

[4] Gibbons v. Ogden, 22 U.S. (9 Wheat.) 1, 196 (1824); Stoutenburgh v. Hennick, 129 U.S. 141 (1889); Atlantic Cleaners & Dyers v. United States, 286 U.S. 427 (1932); In re Bryant, 4 Fed. Cas. 514 (No. 2067) (D. Oreg. 1865); Hanley v. Kansas City Southern Ry. Co., 187 U.S. 617 (1903); Western Union Tel. Co. v. Speight, 254 U.S. 17 (1920).

[5] New York v. United States, 505 U.S. 144, 158 (1992) ("The volume of interstate commerce and the range of commonly accepted objects of government regulation have ... expanded considerably in the last 200 years, and the regulatory authority of Congress has expanded along with them. As interstate commerce has become ubiquitous, activities once considered purely local have come to have effects on the national economy, and have accordingly come within the scope of Congress' commerce power.").

[6] United States v. Morrison, 529 U.S. 598, 617 (2000); United States v. Lopez, 514 U.S. 549, 561 (1995) ("[the] criminal statute [] by its own terms has nothing to do with 'commerce' or any sort of economic enterprise ... [and] is not an essential part of a larger regulation of economic activity, in which the regulatory scheme could be undercut unless the intrastate activity were regulated. It cannot, therefore, be sustained under our cases upholding regulations of activities that arise out of or are connected with a commercial transaction, which viewed in the aggregate, substantially affect interstate commerce.").

[7] Id. at 558-59 (citations omitted).

[8] Id. at 561.

[9] Quoting, id. at 549.

[10] U.S. CONST art. I, § 8, cl. 4. One important difference between the Commerce Clause and the Bankruptcy Clause, is that laws passed under by the Bankruptcy Clause must be uniform. Railway Labor Executives' Assn. v. Gibbons, 455 U.S. 457, 465 (1981). The Court in Gibbons held that a bankruptcy statute that applied to only one debtor was not uniform. Id. at 471. The court also explained the difficulty in: [d]istinguishing a congressional exercise of power under the Commerce Clause from an exercise under the Bankruptcy clause ... Although we have noted that the subject of bankruptcies is incapable of final definition, we have previously defined "bankruptcy" as the subject of the relations between an insolvent or nonpaying or fraudulent debtor and his creditors, extending to his and their relief. Congress' power under the Bankruptcy Clause contemplates an adjustment of a failing debtor's obligations This power extends to all cases where the law causes to be distributed, the property of the debtors among his creditors. It includes the power to discharge the debtor from his contracts and legal liabilities, as well as to distribute this property. The grant to Congress involves the power to impair the obligation of contracts, and this the States were forbidden to do. Id. at 466 (internal citations and quotations omitted).

[11] Hanover Nat'l Bank v. Moyses, 186 U.S. 181 (1938); In re Klein, 42 U.S. (1 How) 277 (1843).

[12] This deference probably would increase the foreseeability of a statutorily imposed interest rate freeze/reduction, which is important to an analysis under the "impairment of investment-backed expectations" prong of the takings test that a court is likely to apply to the legislation in question. For more information on this prong, see the "Impairment of

Investment-Backed Expectations" subsection of the "Application of Penn Central to an Interest Rate Freeze/Reduction" section of this report.

[13] Measures, such as H.R. 3609 (the Emergency Home Ownership and Mortgage Equity Protection Act, as it was ordered to be reported favorably by the House Judiciary Committee) likely would be a valid extension of Congress's authority to pass uniform laws on bankruptcies because those bills seek to amend how certain debts secured by the debtor's primary residence are dealt with in a Chapter 13 bankruptcy reorganization plan. It is less clear if a piece of legislation that places an interest rate freeze/reduction on all mortgages originated nationwide or a certain group of mortgages that are not in default or delinquent could be passed pursuant to Congress's bankruptcy authority. For more information on H.R. 3609 and similar bills, see CRS Report RL3430 1, The Primary Residence Exception: Legislative Proposals in the 110th Congress to Amend Section 1322 (b) (2) of the Bankruptcy Code, by David H. Carpenter.

[14] For an example of how the Supreme Court has analyzed state impairment of contracts, see Home Building and Loan Assoc. v. Blaisdell, 290 U.S. 398 (1934) (upholding a state statute that imposed a foreclosure moratorium on certain properties).

[15] PBGC v. R.A. Gray & Co., 467 U.S. 717, 733 (1984). Accord, United States v. Winstar Corp., 518 U.S. 839, 875-76 (1996).

[16] PBGC, 467 U.S. at 733.

[17] Torromeo v. Town of Fremont, N.H., 438 F.3d 113, 118 (1st Cir. 2006). Prior to 2005, there was a great deal of confusion among courts in how to properly delineate between takings law and substantive due process analysis, which was partially alleviated by the Supreme Court's 2005 Lingle v. Chevron U.S.A. Inc. decision. 544 U.S. 528 (2005). See, e.g., Agins v. City of Tiburon, 447 U.S. 255 (1980); Kavanau v. Santa Monica Rent Control Bd., 941 P.2d 851 (Cal. 1997). While some confusion remains, the Court has clarified that substantive due process and takings law address unique concerns.

[18] See, e.g., Eastern Enterprises v. Apfel, 524 U.S. 498 (1998).

[19] It also is possible for one to claim an Equal Protection Clause violation, especially if the claimant believes that she was treated unequally. See, e.g., Village of Willowbrook v. Olech, 528 U.S. 562 (2000). An Equal Protection Clause violation is not likely to result from an interest rate freeze/reduction that is not limited to members of a protected class, such as race or ethnicity.

[20] Mortgages and the contract rights to mortgage-backed securities investments are private property for the purpose of Fifth Amendment protections.

[21] Lingle, 544 U.S. at 538.

[22] Id.

[23] 506 U.S. 1003 (1992).

[24] Lingle, 544 U.S. at 538.

[25] See, e.g., Hawkeye Commodity Promotions, Inc. v. Vilsack, 486 F.3d 430, 441 (8th Cir. 2007) ("it appears that Lucas[' total takings test] protects real property only"); Unity Real Estate v. Hudson, 178 F.3d 649, 674 (3rd Cir. 1999) ("To date, the categorical approach has only been used in real property cases such as Lucas v. South Carolina ...."). However, at least one Federal Circuit case has applied total takings analysis to personal property, though it did not find a taking had occurred. Maritrans v. United States, 342 F.3d 1344 (Fed. Cir. 2003).

[26] Lingle, 544 U.S. at 538.

[27] 438 U.S. 104 (1978) (the Court found no taking where New York City, pursuant to a historic preservation ordinance, prevented a property owner from developing the air rights over a historic landmark). See also, Lingle 544 U.S. at 538-39.

[28] Robert Meltz, Takings Law Today: A Primer for the Perplexed, 34 Ecology L.Q. 307, 364-65 (2007).

[29] For more information regarding the securitization process and provisions of typical PSAs, see CRS Report RS22722, Securitization and Federal Regulation of Mortgages for Safety and Soundness, by Edward Vincent Murphy, and CRS Report RL34372, The HOPE NOW Alliance/American Securitization Forum (ASF) Plan to Freeze Certain Mortgage Interest Rates, by David H. Carpenter and Edward Vincent Murphy.

[30] 300 U.S. 440 (1937).

[31] 295 U.S. 555 (1934).

[32] See id. at 598-99.

[33] Id. at 589-90.

[34] Vinton Branch, 300 U.S. at 456-57 (internal citations ommited).

[35] Id. at 470.

[36] Id.

[37] As one court explained, "whether or not Louisville Joint Stock Land Bank v. Radford has any current value as precedent is subject to

reasonable doubt. Times have changed, and a review of its progeny discloses a constant and steady erosion of its vitality." In re Pommerer, 10 B.R. 935, 945 (Bankr. Ct. D. Minn. 1981). However, neither case has been formally overruled, and some lower courts have cited both within the last 20 years.

[38] Radford, 555 U.S. at 601 (emphasis added).

[39] Vinton Branch, 300 U.S. at 470 (emphasis added).

[40] Lingle, 544 U.S. at 542-43 ("The 'substantially advances' formula suggests a means-ends test: It asks, in essence, whether a regulation of private property is effective in achieving some legitimate public purpose. An inquiry of this nature has some logic in the context of a due process challenge, for a regulation that fails to serve any legitimate governmental objective may be so arbitrary or irrational that it runs afoul of the Due Process Clause. But such a test is not a valid method of discerning whether private property has been 'taken' for purposes of the Fifth Amendment.... A test that tells us nothing about the actual burden imposed on property rights, or how that burden is allocated, cannot tell us when justice might require that the burden be spread among taxpayers through the payment of compensation. The owner of a property subject to a regulation that effectively serves a legitimate state interest may be just as singled out and just as burdened as the owner of a property subject to an ineffective regulation. It would make little sense to say that the second owner has suffered a taking while the first has not. Likewise, an ineffective regulation may not significantly burden property rights at all, and it may distribute any burden broadly and evenly among property owners. The notion that such a regulation nevertheless 'takes' private property for public use merely by virtue of its ineffectiveness or foolishness is untenable." (emphasis original) (internal citations omitted)).

[41] Id. at 548 (citing Nollan v. California Coastal Comm'n, 483 U.S. 825 (1997), and Dolan v. City of Tigard, 512 U.S. 374 (1994)).

[42] Penn Central, 438 U.S. at 124.

[43] It should be noted that the Supreme Court has indicated that government actions that are implemented for a public benefit and only incidentally interfere with the performance of private contracts constitute only a frustration, not a taking, of contract rights. Omnia Commercial Co. v. United States, 261 U.S. 502 (1923). The legislative issue this report is addressing, on the other hand, would directly target private mortgage contracts, as opposed to incidentally interfering with the contracts. When

legislation specifically targets an existing contract or a class of contracts, the courts have found that Omnia does not apply, and instead have applied Penn Central's balancing test. See, Cienega Gardens v. United States, 331 F.3d. 1319, 1335 (Fed. Cir. 2003) ("Omnia ... refers to legislation targeted at some public benefit, which incidentally affects contract rights, not ... legislation aimed at the contract rights themselves in order to nullify them.").

[44] Penn Central, 438 U.S. at 124-28; Pennsylvania Coal Co. v. Mahon, 260 U.S. 393, 415 (1922); Nollan v. California Coastal Comm'n, 483 U.S. 825, 834 (1985).

[45] Lingle, 544 U.S. at 539.

[46] Lingle, 544 U.S. at 540.

[47] The parcel as a whole concept was originally established, as was most of Takings Clause jurisprudence, for land-use takings claims. The courts have extended the parcel as a whole concept to contexts other than land-use, such as employee pension plans, Concrete Pipe & Products, Inc. v. Construction Laborers Pension Trust, 508 U.S. 602, 644 (1993), and mortgage restrictions on low-income housing projects, Cienega Gardens v. United States, 503 F.3d 1266 (Fed. Cir. 2007).

[48] Concrete Pipe, 508 U.S. at 644.

[49] Andrus v. Allard, 444 U.S. 51, 66 (1979), cited in Tahoe-Sierra Pres. Council, Inc. v. Tahoe Reg'l Planning Agency, 535 U.S. 302, 327 (2002).

[50] Tahoe-Sierra, 535 U.S. at 33 1-32.

[51] Rose Acre Farm, Inc. v. United States, 75 Fed. Cl. 527, 532 (2007). Other courts have looked to whether only a small number of many contractual rights are affected by the regulation. See, McAndrews v. Fleet Bank of Massachusetts, 989 F.2d 13, 18-19 (1st Cir. 1993). However, this type of analysis would not fit well in the context of a takings claim raised by an investor of MBSs.

[52] See, Concrete Pipe, 508 U.S. at 645.

[53] See, e.g., Appolo Fuels, Inc. v. United States, 381 F.3d 1338 (Fed. Cir. 2004). For this purpose, the courts examine the regulations in place before the plaintiff acquired the property in question.

[54] Cienega Gardens, 503 F.3d at 1289.

[55] Branch v. United States, 69 F.3d 1571, 1581 (Fed. Cir. 1995).

[56] Concrete Pipe, 508 U.S. at 645-46.

[57] Other "heavily regulated fields include: railroad labor disputes (Burlington N.R.R. Co. v. United Transp. Union, 822 F. Supp. 797, 802

(D.D.C. 1991)); coal mining (Appolo Fuels, 381 F.3d, at 1349); liquor stores (People's Super Liquor Stores, Inc. v. Jenkins, 432 F. Supp.2d 200, 215 (D. Mass. 2006)); gambling (Hawkeye Commodity Promotions, 486 F.3d at 440); and adult entertainment establishments (McCrothers Corp. v. City of Mandan, 728 N.W.2d 124, 141 (N.D. 2007)).

[58] Cienega Gardens, 503 F.3d, at 1289.

[59] For more information on Congress's powers pursuant to the Bankruptcy Clause, see the "Legislative Authority to Pass an Interest Rate Freeze/Reduction" section of this report.

[60] 544 U.S. at 542 ("The 'substantially advances' formula suggests a means-ends test: It suggests, in essence, whether a regulation of private property is effective in achieving some legitimate public purpose. An inquiry of this nature has some logic in the context of a due process challenge . . . But such a test is not a valid method of discerning whether private property has been "taken" for purposes of the Fifth Amendment.") (emphasis in original).

[61] See, e.g., Tahoe-Sierra Preservation Council, Inc. v. Tahoe Regional Planning Agency, 535 U.S. at 333 (were it not for findings that the agency acted in good faith, the Court "might have concluded the agency was stalling" and found a taking).

[62] A facial challenge would not succeed under Penn Central because the particular facts of plaintiffs' property would be pivotal to a regulatory takings analysis. A facial challenge would be possible if the court found an interest rate freeze/reduction to be a physical taking. See, the "Physical Taking/Appropriation vs. Regulatory Taking" section of this report.

[63] The value of securitized mortgages was around $2 trillion in 2006. See, CRS Report RS22722, Securitization and Federal Regulation of Mortgages for Safety and Soundness, by Edward Vincent Murphy.

In: Understanding Mortgage Meltdowns
Editor: A. V. Carey
ISBN: 978-1-60692-789-2

Chapter 6

SUBPRIME MORTGAGES: PRIMER ON CURRENT LENDING AND FORECLOSURE ISSUES*

Edward Vincent Murphy

ABSTRACT

Subprime mortgages are loans extended to borrowers with weak credit profiles. Subprime mortgages entail higher risk of delinquency and default. Recent increases in subprime borrower foreclosures and lender bankruptcies have prompted concerns that some lenders' underwriting guidelines are too loose and that some borrowers may not have fully understood the risks of the mortgage products they chose. Regulatory agencies are revisiting the guidance they provide lenders and are reevaluating required disclosures to consumers. In addition, Congress is holding hearings on the subject and may consider consumer protection legislation.

Subprime foreclosures have reached the highs of the 2000-200 1 recession but delinquency rates are not the same across mortgage features. The adjustable interest rate (ARM) feature is currently associated with higher delinquency rates than comparable fixed rate loans. However, the delinquency rate of loans with the negative amortization (NegAm) feature has remained below 1%,

* This is an edited, excerpted and augmented edition of a Congressional Research Service Publication RL33930, dated March 19, 2007.

the range normally associated with less risky loans. NegAm is a loan that allows a monthly payment less than the current interest on the loan with the remaining interest added to the principal, thus increasing the loan balance.

Financial regulators issued a guidance for alternative mortgage products in October 2006 and issued a proposed statement for subprime lending in March 2007. The guidances require that consumers be given plain-language explanations of the risks of their mortgages. Borrowers must be qualified for mortgage loans based on the ability to repay the loan, not based on speculation about future increases in the value of the real estate collateral. The proposed guidance also seeks to limit payment shock and prepayment penalties. Policymakers are faced with the challenge of balancing the benefits of access to credit against the costs of potential foreclosures.

This report will be updated in the event of significant regulatory or legislative change.

BACKGROUND

Subprime mortgage lending can benefit consumers by allowing greater access to credit, and thus homeownership, but can also impose costs on consumers through defaults and foreclosures. Subprime refers to people who have no credit history, have a blemished credit record, and/or have a weak debt-service-to-income ratio. A generation ago, subprime loan applicants were generally denied credit and neither enjoyed homeownership nor risked default. Policymakers evaluating subprime lending issues will be called on to consider the benefits of increased access to credit markets which can lead to homeownership as well as the costs of increased debt burdens and potential foreclosure. To that end, this report describes the subprime market, presents delinquency and foreclosure data, and summarizes banking agency guidance on subprime lending.

The rise of risk-based pricing encouraged growth of the subprime market during the mid-1990s.[1] For example, the number of subprime refinance loans increased nearly tenfold between 1993 and 1998.[2] Subprime loans increased from an estimated 5% of the mortgage market in 1994 to as much as 20% in 2005.[3] After retreating during the recession of 1999-2001, subprime lending expanded rapidly during 2002- 2005. In 2006, the housing market slowed and there was a rise in late mortgage payments and foreclosures. The rise in delinquencies and foreclosures continues to be more severe in the subprime market than the prime market but both rates are growing. Several prominent subprime lenders are experiencing financial difficulties, including the recent bankruptcy of Ownit and investigations into New Century. Potential negative consequences for consumers, banks, and financial markets have drawn renewed attention to government policies related to subprime lending.

Government policies play a role at each stage of the mortgage lending process. When a borrower takes out a mortgage loan, the Truth in Lending Act (TILA) and the Home Ownership Equity Protection Act (HOEPA) provide rules for disclosure and limitations on the terms of certain high cost loans. When lenders originate loans, the regulatory agencies of the Federal Financial Institutions Examinations Council (FFIEC) supervise their portfolios to ensure safe and sound banking practices.[4] When lenders sell some of their loans to secondary markets through the government sponsored enterprises (GSEs), Fannie Mae and Freddie Mac, the Office of Federal Housing Enterprise Oversight (OFHEO) supervises the GSEs for safety and soundness and the Department of Housing and Urban Development (HUD) regulates the GSE's charter compliance. When investors purchase mortgage-backed securities (MB S) issued by the GSEs or their competitors, the Securities and Exchange Commission (SEC) enforces the anti-fraud provisions of the securities laws.

Government policies designed to aid lower-income consumers achieve homeownership may have contributed to the expansion of subprime lending. For example, the Community Reinvestment Act (CRA) encourages lenders to provide loans in the poorer areas of their market where subprime borrowers are more likely to reside. Similarly, increases in HUD's Affordable Housing Goals encourage the GSEs to expand their purchases of loans originated from lower-income and minority borrowers who are more likely to be subprime. Federal Housing Administration (FHA) slowness to adopt some of the nontraditional mortgage products that became popular when house prices were rising rapidly may have resulted in some FHA- eligible borrowers turning to subprime lenders.

THE SUBPRIME MARKET AND ALTERNATIVE MORTGAGES

Generally, subprime mortgages are defined in terms of the credit bureau risk score (FICO) of the borrower.[5] Other credit imperfections, however, can also cause borrowers to be categorized as subprime for a particular loan. For example, the addition of the mortgage loan might increase the borrower's debt-to-income level above traditionally prudent thresholds. Generally, bank supervisors look for one or more of the following credit-risk characteristics when deciding to label a loan subprime:[6]

Recent payment delinquencies (30-day or 60-day depending on recency)
Judgment, foreclosure, repossession, or charge-off within prior two years
Bankruptcy in the last five years
Relatively high default probability (FICO below 660 or similar measure)
Limited ability to cover living expenses after debts (debt-service-to-income ratio of 50% or more)

Subprime loans are disproportionately used by the elderly and members of minority groups. The elderly are more likely to own a home and to have accumulated significant equity and therefore are more likely to qualify for a refinance loan despite, perhaps, having imperfect credit. Minorities, on average, have lower incomes and therefore are often more likely to have credit blemishes. In addition, there is some evidence that minorities who could qualify for cheaper prime loans are sometimes borrowing in the more expensive subprime market.[7]

In recent years, subprime borrowers increasingly used alternative mortgage products that had previously been used primarily by sophisticated investors. Interest only (I-O) mortgages provide an introductory period during which monthly payments cover only the loan interest. After the introductory period, loan payments reset to a higher amount to also cover the loan's principal. Negative amortizing mortgages (NegAms) allow borrowers to pay less than current interest due and result in a higher loan balance and higher future payments. In contrast to fixed rate mortgages (FRM), which have fixed interest rates and constant monthly payments, adjustable rate mortgages (ARMs) reset the interest rate with changes in market interest rates and therefore can result in higher or lower monthly payments depending on market conditions. Because alternative mortgage products allow monthly payments to rise, some policymakers are concerned that subprime borrowers in particular may not have fully understood the risks associated with non-traditional features.

Growth, Foreclosures, and Risk in Subprime Mortgages

Expansion of the subprime market may have benefited some consumers by improving access to credit and facilitating homeownership. The timing of the growth of the subprime market corresponds to growth in homeownership. The U.S. homeownership rate increased from 64.1% in 1993 to 68.9% in 2005.[8]

Homeownership among minority groups increased at a faster rate, from 42.4% in 1993 to 5 1.3% in 2005. Recall that subprime lending is more prevalent in minority communities. The homeownership gap between white-non-hispanics and all-minorities dropped from 27.8 percentage points in 1993 to 24.5 percentage points in 2005.

Expansion of the subprime market may have increased the costs associated with greater debt burdens. Subprime foreclosures increased faster than prime foreclosures during the 2000-200 1 recession and are again rising faster than prime foreclosures in the current housing slowdown. Figure 1 presents data from the Mortgage Bankers Association mortgage delinquency survey. Subprime loans in this sample are several times more likely to go into foreclosure and are far more sensitive to the credit cycle than prime loans. Figure 1 shows that less than 1% of prime loans were in foreclosure during 1998-2006. In contrast, at least 3% of subprime loans were generally in foreclosure. During the 2000-200 1 recession, subprime foreclosures reached almost 10%. In the current housing downturn, subprime foreclosures are again rising rapidly.

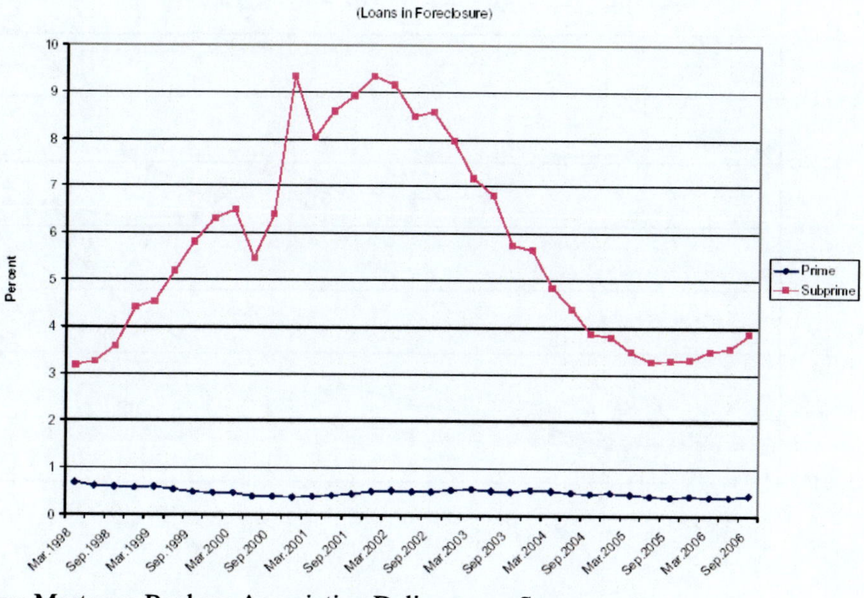

Source: Mortgage Bankers Association Delinquency Survey.

Figure 1. Prime and Subprime Loans in Foreclosure, 1998-2006.

In Figure 2, the composite categories have been further separated into fixed rate mortgage (FRM) foreclosures and adjustable rate mortgage (ARM) foreclosures. From 2006 to the fourth quarter of 2007, the subprime foreclosure rates are again the highest, followed by FHA, and then prime loans. The foreclosure rates averaged 3.18% for subprime FRM loans, 7.03% for subprime ARM loans, 1.97% for FHA FRM loans, 2.79% for FHA ARM loans, 0.41% for prime FRM loans, and 1.21% for prime ARM loans. The NDS does not report composite foreclosure rates for all FRM loans or all ARM loans. Based upon the information provided here, however, the overall FRM and ARM composite foreclosure rates are likely to be much lower than the equivalent rates computed for the subprime and FHA categories. Furthermore, the composite series of FRM loan foreclosure rates is likely to be lower than composite series of foreclosure rates for ARM loans.[5] The descriptive data in Figure 2 indicate that many of the foreclosures were associated with ARM loans, in particular, the subprime ARM loans.

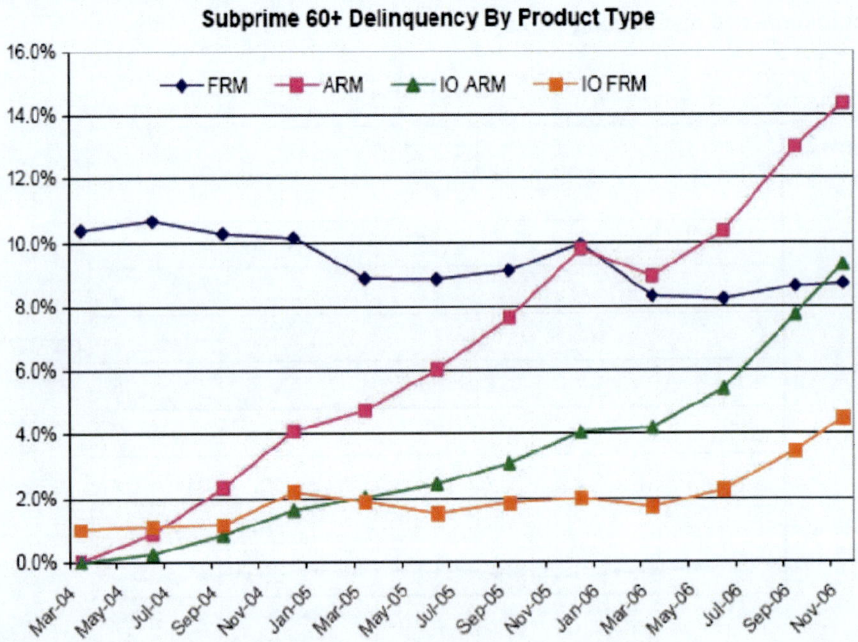

Figure 2. Delinquency Rate of Subprime Mortgages by Feature.

The 60-day delinquency rate for negative amortizing (NegAm) loans is rising but remains relatively low. NegAm loans give the borrower the option of paying less than the interest owed in any month and therefore can increase the loan balance. In the sample analyzed by Loan Performance, most NegAm ARMs originated during 2004-2006 have increased their balance but the delinquency rate for these products has not risen as fast as subprime delinquency rates. The 60-day delinquency rate for all NegAm ARMs originated in 2006 remained below 1%, but the 60-day delinquency rate for subprime ARMs originated in 2006 exceeds 8%.[11]

STRESS ON SUBPRIME LENDERS

In addition to rising foreclosures among subprime borrowers, the slowdown in the housing market has also challenged subprime lenders. Many subprime lenders raise funds by selling their loans to investors in the secondary market and using the proceeds to make new loans. These lenders can suffer significant hardship if investors downgrade the value of subprime debt. For example, Ownit Mortgage declared bankruptcy in December 2006, reportedly after it lost financing from Merrill Lynch and other investors.[12] New Century is under investigation for accounting and other improprieties connected to its subprime business. Several other lenders have shut their doors or restricted their subprime lending.

Stress on subprime financing is not confined to just a few lenders. A key indicator of investor estimation of the risk associated with funding loans through secondary markets, the ABX index, declined suddenly and significantly for subprime loans in February 2007 (see Figure 3). The ABX index is based on the cost of hedging purchases of mortgage loans that are packaged into securities and sold to investors in the secondary market.[13] According to Markit, an independent provider of data for derivatives trades, the price that investors were willing to pay for the BBB- rated portion of the index (part of the subprime market) fell from just over 97% on January 19, 2007, to under 70% by February 26, 2007.[14] The decline in the ABX index reflects the reduced willingness of investors to accept the risks associated with subprime loans. As a result, funds for additional subprime loans are decreasing.

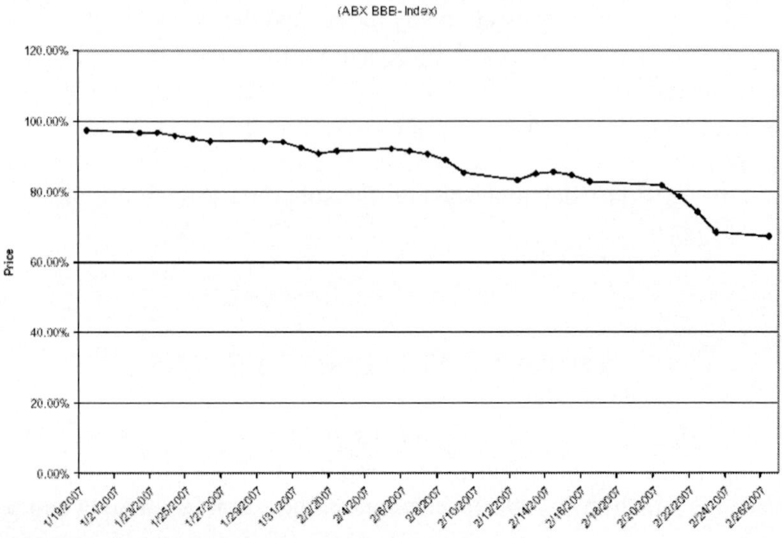

Source: Markit Group Limited.

Figure 3. ABX Index of BBB- Rated Mortgage Derivatives.

The safety and soundness of subprime lenders has been a concern for many policymakers because some believe that disruptions in financial markets could have wider effects on the economy. For example, some believe that banking disruptions can make the business cycle more volatile. Federal responses to the Savings and Loan Crisis in the 1980s may have been due in part to concerns for the larger economy. The Federal Reserve itself was created because of a congressional commission to study banking issues in the Panic of 1907. While disruptions in the current subprime market do not rise to the level of historic banking panics, financial regulatory agencies have made public their intention to closely watch the subprime sector. The FFIEC agencies have issued new inter-agency guidance "to address emerging issues and questions relating to certain subprime mortgage lending practices."[15]

BANKING AGENCY GUIDANCE

Financial regulators have recognized the increased risks of subprime lending. Rising subprime foreclosures during 2000 prompted the OCC to tighten oversight of subprime lending programs in January 2001. "Institutions with significant subprime lending activities will be subject to closer scrutiny to ensure that their programs have appropriate risk management controls and capital support."[16] The guidance covered capital maintenance, standards for individual loan review by examiners, documentation requirements for delinquent subprime accounts, and policies to curb potentially abusive lending practices.

Since 2001, as mortgage markets have continued to evolve, and housing markets have expanded, subprime lending has drawn renewed attention. In October 2006, the lending regulators of the FFIEC issued guidance for alternative mortgage products. The guidance reiterated that lenders must qualify loans based on the borrower's ability to repay the loan balance, not based on the value of the loan collateral in sale or foreclosure. The October 2006 guidance also reminded lenders of Truth in Lending Act requirements to explain payment terms in plain language in order to curb abusive lending practices.

With subprime delinquencies and foreclosures mounting again, the FFIEC has issued a new interagency guidance for comment. The proposed guidance "reiterates many of the principles addressed in existing guidance relative to prudent risk management practices and consumer protection laws."[17] Concerning risk management, the proposed guidance states that predatory lending typically involves at least one of (1) lending on collateral value rather than borrower ability to repay, (2) inducing repeated refinances to charge high points and fees, or (3) using deceptive marketing to conceal the true nature of the mortgage obligation. Concerning consumer protection, the proposed guidance states that mortgage product descriptions and advertisements should provide clear, detailed information on the costs, terms, features, and risks of the loan to the borrower, including any payment shock or prepayment penalty.

In the proposed guidance, the FFIEC asks for comments concerning restrictions on planned refinances because "the structural evolution of subprime mortgage lending in recent years has introduced some products that are intended at their outset to be temporary credit accommodations in anticipation of early sale or refinancing, rather than longer-term amortizing accounts."[18] Commentors are asked to address the following:

Do planned subprime refinances always present inappropriate risks that should be discouraged? If not, under what circumstances are they appropriate?

Will the proposed guidance restrict existing subprime borrowers' attempts to refinance and avoid payment shock?

Should restrictions on planned refinances apply beyond subprime markets?

Should prepayment penalties be restricted to the introductory period?

POLICY CONSIDERATIONS

Subprime loans, which are extended to borrowers with weaker credit conditions, have higher delinquency and foreclosure rates. Policies that facilitate subprime lending have to balance the benefits of homeownership against the risks of increased debt. More complex mortgage products may facilitate homeownership under some conditions but may be more difficult for consumers to understand.[19] Restrictions on mortgage products may insulate credit-impaired borrowers from default risk but may make it more difficult for these potential borrowers to own a home. Federal and state authorities also protect consumers through anti-predatory lending initiatives.[20] The recent rise in subprime delinquencies illustrates the trade-off between encouraging greater access to credit markets and risking increased defaults and foreclosures.

Policymakers decide the role of government agencies and government sponsored enterprises (GSEs) in the subprime sector.[21] Some argue that greater GSE presence in the subprime market could help reduce instability in that market by helping to standardize underwriting procedures. Raising the GSEs' housing goals may direct their programs to lower-income households but may increase the flow of funds to risky mortgages.[22] Reforming the loan programs of the Federal Housing Administration (FHA) could provide lower-income borrowers with an alternative to subprime lenders but may be less flexible in changing market conditions.[23] FHA makes it easier for borrowers to obtain loans by insuring the loan payments. On the other hand, some argue that granting FHA greater flexibility could increase the amount of risky mortgages.

REFERENCES

[1] Risk-based pricing refers to assessing a borrower's risk and then charging higher-risk borrowers a higher interest rate rather than simply refusing to qualify them for a loan. In contrast, pool-based pricing accepts a range of borrowers into a pool which is charged the same rate based

on the average credit quality of the pool. Borrowers outside the pool are simply denied credit.

[2] "Unequal Burden in New York: Income and Racial Disparities in Subprime Lending," Department of Housing and Urban Development (HUD), May 2000, p.1. The study cites the Home Mortgage Disclosure Act (HMDA) database as reporting 80,000 subprime loans in 1993 and 790,000 in 1998.

[3] Robert Avery et al., "Higher-Priced Home Lending and the 2005 HMDA Data," Federal Reserve Bulletin, September, 2006 (rev.), p. A125. There is no single accepted source for subprime market share. The Federal Reserve collects loan information through the Home Mortgage Disclosure Act (HMDA), which does not currently require lenders to report a borrower's credit score and only requires interest rate information if the rate is more than 3% above a comparable Treasury rate. The proportion of loans that exceed HMDA's 3% threshold, and are thus considered high cost, is sensitive to changes in the proportion of loans that are adjustable rate and to the difference between short-term and long-term interest rates. Alternatively, the Department of Housing and Urban Development maintains a list of lenders who specialize in loans to consumers with weaker credit. The market share of these lenders can vary significantly over time. Private financial consultants with access to more detailed lender loan information provide a third set of estimates.

[4] The FFIEC includes the Federal Reserve Board (FRB), the Federal Deposit Insurance Corporation (FDIC), The Office of Thrift Supervision (OTS), the Office of the Comptroller of the Currency (OCC), and the National Credit Union Administration (NCUA).

[5] A FICO score is an estimate of a borrowers creditworthiness provided by credit rating agencies that monitor consumer payment histories. The term comes from the company, Fair Isaacs, that originated the score and continues to provide it to lenders.

[6] "Subprime Lending (Risk Management and Internal Controls)," *Bank Holding Company (BHC) Supervision Manual*, Section 2128.08, Dec. 2002, pp1-2.

[7] Unequal Burden: Income and Racial Disparities in Subprime Lending in America, HUD, 2000.

[8] U.S. Department of Commerce, Bureau of the Census. The year 1993 is chosen as the beginning point both because Census data reflect a

changed weighting procedure in that year and because the subprime market grew rapidly during 1993-1998.

[9] A fully amortizing loan pays off the loan balance using the traditional method of constant monthly payments. An interest-only loan has an introductory period of lower payments during which the monthly payments do not pay down the loan balance.

[10] Loan Performance calculations cited in *Economic Commentary*, Fannie Mae, February 20, 2007, p.2. A 60-day delinquent loan is not yet a loan in foreclosure. Loan Performance's definition of subprime does not necessarily match the Mortgage Bankers Association survey.

[11] Loan Performance calculations cited in *Economic Commentary*, Fannie Mae, February 20, 2007, p.2. Not all subprime loans are NegAm loans and not all NegAm loans are subprime loans.

[12] Julie Creswell and Vikas Baj aj, "A Mortgage Crisis Begins to Spiral and Casualties Mount," *New York Times*, Mar. 5, 2007, p. C1.

[13] Investors can use insurance and other financial instruments to reduce their exposure to the risk that their investment will go sour. A traditional hedge occurs when someone simultaneously invests in two instruments that move in opposite directions so that if one goes bad, the other partially compensates. The ABX index is one measure of the price investors are willing to pay to hedge mortgage backed securities.

[14] Data provided by Markit Group, Limited. The company receives daily data contributions from over 70 firms dealing in related securities. See [http://www.Markit.com]. A decline in the index percentage represents an increase in the cost to hedge the investment.

[15] "Proposed Statement on Subprime Mortgage Lending," Federal Register, Vol 72, No. 45, Mar. 8, 2007, p. 10533.

[16] "Subprime Lending: Expanded Guidance for Subprime Lending Programs," OCC 2001-6, Jan. 31, 2001. This bulletin supplements OCC Bulletin 1999-15, "Subprime Lending, Risks and Rewards."

[17] "Proposed Statement on Subprime Mortgage Lending," Federal Register, Vol 72, No. 45, Mar. 8, 2007, p. 10533.

[18] "Proposed Statement on Subprime Mortgage Lending," Federal Register, Vol 72, No. 45, Mar. 8, 2007, p. 10533.

[19] CRS Report RL33775, Alternative Mortgages: Risks to Consumers and Lenders in the Current Housing Cycle, by Edward Vincent Murphy.

[20] CRS Report RL3 27 84, Predatory Lending: A Comparison of State Laws to the Federal Home Ownership and Equity Protection Act, by Kamilah M. Holder, Kate M. Manuel.

[21] CRS Report RS22336, *GSE Reform: A New Affordable Housing Fund*, by N. Eric Weiss.

[22] The GSE housing goals refer to the percentage of housing units financed by the GSEs' loan purchases that must be for low income groups and underserved areas. The housing goals are set by HUD.

[23] CRS Report RS20530, *FHA Loan Insurance Program: An Overview*, by Bruce E. Foote, Meredith Peterson.

In: Understanding Mortgage Meltdowns
Editor: A. V. Carey
ISBN: 978-1-60692-789-2

Chapter 7

GOVERNMENT INTERVENTIONS IN FINANCIAL MARKETS: ECONOMIC AND HISTORIC ANALYSIS OF SUBPRIME MORTGAGE OPTIONS*

N. Eric Weiss

ABSTRACT

This report summarizes and analyzes four previous government market interventions (Home Owners Loan Corporation in 1933, Continental Illinois in 1984, the savings and loan insurance fund shortfall in 1989, and the Latin American debt crisis in 1989), in light of current mortgage market conditions. Current proposals to help delinquent homeowners share many features in common with all of these actions.

The Home Owners Loan Corporation (HOLC) purchased delinquent mortgages at a discount and worked with homeowners to restructure the mortgages into more manageable terms. HOLC accepted slightly more than one million applications from homeowners to refinance their homes between June 1933 and June 1935. It rejected 488,000 applications, most for "inadequate security" and "lack of distress." HOLC foreclosed on 194,000 of those it was attempting to assist. At the time, many had serious concern that HOLC could be a costly undertaking, but when it disbanded in the early 1 950s, HOLC returned a

* This is an edited, excerpted and augmented edition of a Congressional Research Service Publication RL34423, dated April 18, 2008.

small profit to the government. HOLC successfully conceived and implemented new ways to contact delinquent homeowners and, in some cases, help homeowners find new jobs.

In 1984, Continental Illinois National Bank suffered a run after loans that it had not properly underwritten failed. The Federal Reserve and the Federal Deposit Insurance Corporation led intervention efforts. There were concerns that allowing the bank to fail could have serious repercussions throughout the financial system. This led to the FDIC Improvement Act of 1991.

In the 1 980s, the Federal Savings and Loan Insurance Corporation approached insolvency because of the failure of member savings and loan institutions, also known as thrifts. Working together, Congress and the George H. W. Bush administration established the Resolution Trust Corporation (RTC), which was funded by the Resolution Funding Corporation (REFCORP). The thrift industry is still paying off the intervention operation, which is estimated to have cost $152.9 billion.

In 1989, Brady bonds helped less developed countries, mostly in Latin America, restructure their debt by renegotiating terms and writing down some of the loans. The plan, proposed by then-U.S. Treasury Secretary Nicholas F. Brady, overcame coordination problems in previous restructuring efforts. In addition to writing down some loans, the plan included some interest rate reductions, and having debtor nations post U.S. Treasury bonds as collateral with the Federal Reserve. Approximately $91.8 billion was refinanced under the plan. Repayment continues today.

INTRODUCTION

Increasing delinquency and default rates on subprime mortgages in 2007 and 2008, along with liquidity problems in other financial sectors, have led some to call on the federal government to intervene in the mortgage market. The Administration and the mortgage industry have developed an approach called HOPE NOW that works with borrowers with subprime mortgages facing interest rate increases and increasing payments who could be helped with a combination of counseling and either an interest rate freeze or a new mortgage.[1] Critics of the plan believe that HOPE NOW is doing too little, too slowly to help those in need today and those who will face interest rate increases over the next few years.[2]

Foreclosure is costly for the lender, the borrower, and owners of neighboring property. Efforts to reduce foreclosures could very well be in the interest of all three affected parties. In foreclosure the lender is unlikely to recover the outstanding balance on the mortgage and the cost of foreclosure. The borrower is likely to lose any equity in the home, incur additional costs, and suffer credit impairment. A large number of vacant homes in a neighborhood can reduce the value of occupied homes. This spillover from the borrower and mortgage holder of the vacant homes to the neighbors is an example of what economists term an externality and provides a possible economic rationale for government intervention.

Some analysts and journalists have drawn a parallel between the delinquency and default problems facing homeowners with subprime mortgages and distressed homeowners during the Great Depression.[3] The Home Owners' Loan Corporation (HOLC) was created in 1933 to refinance homeowners' mortgages. This report analyzes HOLC, the Continental Illinois failure and government reaction in 1984, the savings and loan crisis of the 1 980s, and the 1989 Brady Plan for bonds from developing countries.

POLICY ISSUES

One of the first issues that Congress may choose to consider when contemplating an intervention is which home owners should be included in the plan. When there is a limited amount of aid, how should it be divided? At the one extreme, if assistance goes to only a few, those who obtain it may receive more assistance than is necessary or some in identical situations could be excluded. At the other extreme, if the assistance goes to a large number, there is a risk of spreading the help too thinly to be of assistance, or those who do not need help may receive it.

In short, who "deserves" to be helped? For example, should owners of rental property be assisted or only present owners? Should vacation and other second homes be included? Should persons with two homes who are trying to sell one be aided? Should owners of any type of housing be helped or just owners of singlefamily housing?[4]

If only one group, such as owners with subprime mortgages, is to be helped, should this group be further divided? For example, should those current on their mortgages be assisted? Should those who are behind on their payments be aided? What about those whose mortgage interest rates will reset in the future?

Should borrowers with certain types of mortgages be excluded? For example, should those with no- or low-documentation loans be excluded? Should an owner who made false or fraudulent statements to obtain the mortgage be aided?

Does it matter if the mortgage was obtained to purchase a home as opposed to refinancing the home? If refinancings are to be included, should there be a limit to the amount of cash equity that the borrower extracted from the house?

Finally, should there be a cutoff date? If there should, should it be a "date certain" or when a certain objective measure is reached?

One response is the HOPE NOW, which is available to homeowners through free telephone consultations with a HUD-approved credit counselor.[5] Its financial assistance is offered only to owner-occupied housing financed by subprime mortgages where the owners are current in their payments, but are not likely to be able to make payments after the mortgage resets. Some of the homeowners accepted by the program will have their mortgage interest rates frozen. Others will be helped to refinance with the Federal Housing Administration (FHA). Homeowners who are delinquent on their mortgage payments may be eligible to refinance in the FHASecure program.[6]

Economists and others worry that any government intervention in market outcomes could lead to the expectation of future intervention. This expectation, called moral hazard, could lead to riskier decisions in the future as home buyers (both those helped and those who did not require aid in the current case) take more risk than they might otherwise do in the expectation that the government will assist them in the future. In turn, this could lead to resources being used in a riskier way than would have occurred without the intervention. Insurance policies usually include deductibles and co-pays to limit moral hazard and to discourage excessive use. The rationale for such standard practices is that because the policy holder would bear part of the financial loss, he or she will exert greater prudence.

A Brief Overview of Subprime Delinquency and Default

In mortgage finance, delinquency occurs when a payment on a loan is overdue. Default occurs when a borrower has failed to meet any of the terms of a mortgage contract, including timely payment. Foreclosure occurs when the lender files to seize the house (collateral) because the borrower is in default. Foreclosure procedures vary from state to state.

Foreclosure is a costly process: one widely cited study estimates that the total cost to a lender of foreclosure, including lost interest, legal fees, and the cost of disposing of the house, is $58,759, and takes an average of 18 months.[7] A more recent report by the staff of the Joint Economic Committee (JEC) estimated the direct loss of property value at $53,493, and the loss of neighborhood property value at an additional $24,163.[8] The JEC estimated that each foreclosure would reduce property tax collections by $692. The JEC estimate did not include legal costs and interest foregone during foreclosure. A Federal Reserve Bank of Chicago report cited an estimate that a lender loses more than $50,000 per foreclosure.[9]

THE NATURE OF THE SUBPRIME RESET PROBLEM

As long as home prices were rising, lenders and borrowers had less need to worry about the ability of the borrower to make payments after a mortgage reset because the mortgage would be refinanced before the reset, and the borrower would profit from the price appreciation.[10] If a borrower could not make the mortgage payments, house price appreciation made certain that the lender was paid and the borrower might also make a profit. One reaction to this was the popularity of no-documentation or low-documentation mortgages in which borrowers supplied little or no information about their financial situations. Another response was the extension of subprime mortgages to borrowers with impaired credit histories. All of these mortgages depended heavily upon home price appreciation to provide repayment in case of foreclosure. Where home prices stop appreciating rapidly, the collateral represented by the home can be insufficient to liquidate the debt without a loss to the lender.

SELECTED PREVIOUS GOVERNMENT INTERVENTIONS

The federal government has intervened in the past to modify market outcomes. In keeping with the current debate on the subprime mortgage actions, this section analyzes in greater detail those previous government actions that directly affected individuals and those that are most relevant to the current discussion on assisting homeowners.

This report examines four government market interventions: (1) the Home Owner Loan Corporation (HOLC) of 1933; (2) Continental Illinois in 1994; (3) the savings and loan crisis of the 1980s; and (4) Brady bonds in 1989. HOLC is included because it has been widely mentioned as a possible model for government action. Continental Illinois, in 1984, is included because the bank failed to properly underwrite loans, and because the Federal Reserve and the Federal Deposit Insurance Corporation led assistance efforts. The savings and loan crisis of the 1980s is included because the problems were closely connected to the financing of homes. Brady bonds are discussed in part because previous attempts to solve the international financial distress failed and also because the comparison between earlier attempts and then-U.S. Treasury Secretary Nicholas F. Brady's proposal might be useful.

Home Owners' Loan Corporation

HOLC was established in 1933 to prevent mortgage foreclosures.[11] Mortgages at that time usually were for three to five years, were generally expected to be renewed, and did not amortize (i.e., were not designed to be paid in full by a series of monthly payments). HOLC exchanged its bonds for mortgages that were in default and mortgages held by financial institutions that were in distress. In HOLC 's first year, the federal guarantee increased from interest only to interest and principal. Mortgages were limited to one- to four-unit structures, with an HOLC-appraised value of $20,000 or less ($321,791 in 2008 dollars), could be for no more than the lesser of $14,000 ($225,254 in 2008 dollars) or 80% of HOLC appraised value, carried a maximum interest rate of 5%, and required monthly amortizing payments for not more than 15 years.[12] The $14,000 maximum mortgage meant that a house worth the maximum value of $20,000 could not have a mortgage for the maximum 80% loan-to-value (LTV) ratio.

HOLC was authorized to issue up to $4.75 billion ($76 billion in 2008 dollars) in bonds that could either be exchanged for defaulted mortgages or for cash. The cash could be used to purchase mortgages from lenders who did not want to take the HOLC bonds. The bonds carried a maximum interest rate of 4% for a maximum of 18 years and were exempt from all state, local, and federal taxes.[13] HOLC lent homeowners money to pay taxes and insurance.

Contemporary Issues

At the time that HOLC was created, some were concerned that lenders would not accept the HOLC bonds. This was addressed by allowing the defaulted mortgages to be purchased for cash and increasing the government guarantee on interest to a federal guarantee on both principal and interest. Today, both private and FHA mortgage insurance guarantee payment of principal and interest.

Results

Not all of those eligible applied, and not all those who applied were eligible. Approximately 40% of those eligible for HOLC mortgages applied and half of these were rejected or withdrawn. Of this 50%, 16% were withdrawn, 18%

were rejected because of inadequate house value, and 13% were rejected for lack of distress.[14]

HOLC employees were not civil servants, and the corporation did not follow federal procurement regulations. Although some forecast that HOLC would lose king a relatively small profit when it was liquidated in 1951, in part because declining interest rates and the government guarantee allowed it to borrow inexpensively.[15] HOLC developed its own mortgage processing and servicing system. It supervised and trained appraisers.

HOLC negotiated flexible repayment terms, but it sought eventual full repayment of the mortgages. It developed new methods of working with borrowers who became delinquent, including personal contact with the borrowers. HOLC would try to find jobs for unemployed homeowners and suggested renting out spare bedrooms. Beginning in 1937, it rewrote loans to make them more affordable. Of the one million loans HOLC issued, it acquired 200,000 homes from borrowers who were unable to pay their mortgages; the national foreclosure rate was 19.4%, but there was wide variation in different states.[16] New York and Massachusetts had foreclosure rates of more than 40%, but foreclosure rates in Michigan, West Virginia, Florida, Montana, Idaho, Wyoming, New Mexico, Nevada, and Oregon were less than 10%.[17] HOLC set the price on the foreclosed homes, included financing, and worked with local real estate agents. At its peak, HOLC had 20,000 employees in 458 offices where applications were accepted.[18]

Although there were provisions to purchase mortgages held at troubled banks, HOLC was designed to work with homeowners.[19] Based on the appraised value, the amount of the new mortgage could be less than the original mortgage, and the lender could take a loss on the mortgage. From an economic point of view, this was providing the lender with financial incentives to mark the mortgage to the current (market) value and to recognize the loss.

Application to Subprime Mortgage Restructuring

A program similar to HOLC could be adopted by Congress. Several questions would need to be answered in applying the lessons from the HOLC to the current situation:

What is the maximum house value that could participate in the program?
What should the maximum loan-to-value ratio be?
What should the maximum term of the loans be?
Should there be any restrictions on the interest rate?
Should the government or the private sector run the program?
How should delinquencies and default by those being assisted be treated?

Should the new organization follow HOLC's experience and help delinquent homeowners find better jobs and rent out spare bedrooms? Should there be a predetermined ending date for the program? If so, should this be a fixed date or one at which some measurable criterion is met?

Continental Illinois

In the first quarter of 1984, Continental Illinois, a major United States money center bank, lost $140 million ($291 million in 2008 dollars) triggering a run by uninsured depositors.[20] The Federal Reserve made secret loans to Continental to provide liquidity and to prop it up. In May 1984, the Federal Deposit Insurance Corporation, the Federal Reserve, and 16 money center banks announced that they would support the uninsured deposits. Additional assistance was required in July 1984. Government assistance totaled $4.5 billion ($9.3 billion in 2008 dollars). The FDIC purchased problem loans at a discount and invested $1 billion ($2 billion in 2008 dollars) in Continental. Continental was re-capitalized giving the federal government 80% of its shares; most of the equity of the shareholders was eliminated.

Contemporary Issues

There was little congressional debate in the Continental case because there was no congressional action required. Observers expressed concern that, by giving a de facto guarantee on uninsured deposits, market discipline was being weakened. Some argued that a bank of Continental's size could not be allowed to fail because failure would impact other U.S. and foreign banks. Some questioned the effectiveness of government bank regulation that allowed Continental to engage in risky lending and incur what were then record losses.

Results

The intervention led to management changes. Bank of America purchased Continental in 1994. Congress passed the FDIC Improvement Act of 1991 to strengthen large bank regulation.[21]

Application to Subprime Mortgage Restructuring

In this case, the Federal Reserve, FDIC, and other banks engaged in the immediate intervention. This appears to be similar to the actions of the Federal Reserve and JP Morgan Chase in the recent intervention leading to the JP

Morgan's purchase of Bear Stearns.[22] Continental had grown rapidly and raised funds by borrowing from other banks (federal funds) and with large, wholesale certificates of deposit (CDs). Continental participated heavily with Penn Square Bank in loans to gas and oil projects. After Penn Square was closed because of defaults on these loans, other banks and CD holders became concerned that Continental might not be able to pay them back. The banks and CD holders refused to roll over their investments.

An analysis by the FDIC concluded that Continental had failed to properly underwrite oil and gas loans made with Penn Square Bank. Many analysts say that subprime lenders also failed to properly underwrite loans, but in this case the loans were to homeowners.

Savings and Loans

In the 1980s, many U.S. savings and loan associations (S&Ls) expanded beyond their traditional business of making mortgages to local home buyers. At the same time, S&L profitability declined because of rising interest rates and a mismatch between maturing of S&L assets and liabilities, resulting in 563 S&L failures between 1980 and 1988.[23] In some cases, fraud, including land "flips," was a factor in S&L failures. The Federal Savings and Loan Insurance Corporation (FSLIC), a federal agency that insured most S&L deposits, became insolvent. Some S&Ls were chartered and guaranteed by states including Ohio and Maryland; these state- sponsored insurers also failed as depositors withdrew their money out of concern for the institutions' financial safety.

Contemporary Issues

Debate centered on estimates of the cost of restructuring the S&L industry and how to pay the cost. There was some concern over forcing high-risk S&Ls out of business.

Results

Congress passed the Financial Institutions Reform, Recovery, and Enforcement Act of 1989 (FIRREA) to "reform, recapitalize, and consolidate" the federal deposit insurance system, but not bail out individuals or lenders.[24] Borrowers were still required to pay their loans. To the extent that federal intervention led to general confidence in the financial markets, consumers benefitted. Congress provided $91.3 billion ($158.7 billion in 2008 dollars) to the Resolution Trust Corporation in order to pay for the restructuring. One of the estimates of the direct and indirect costs to the private and public sectors was $152.9 billion ($191.4 billion in 2008 dollars).[25]

Application to Subprime Mortgage Restructuring

The S&L intervention is included because the problems in the thrift industry were in part due to mortgage lending. However, the purpose of the savings and loan intervention was to minimize the cost to the government of honoring the federal insurance of deposits at illiquid and insolvent savings and loans. Most depositors were not at risk unless the federal government failed to honor its guarantee, and this was not considered. A few depositors were at risk for the amount above $100,000.[26] The intervention was important to the viability of the financial system; the same could be argued for much of the Federal Reserve's recent actions.

Brady Bonds

In 1982, a variety of factors combined to result in problems for Latin American nations trying to repay loans, mostly to U.S. commercial banks. Most observers blame relaxed lending standards, poor debt management by borrower countries, and a changing international economy for the inability of debtor nations to repay their debts.[27] U.S. banks accounted for $91.8 billion ($205.1 billion in 2008 dollars) of $219.4 billion ($490.2 billion in 2008 dollars) lent worldwide to 17 highly indebted countries. Initial attempts by then-U.S. Treasury Secretary James Baker to combine structural economic changes of debtor nations, and debt rescheduling including lengthening maturities did not succeed because of difficulties in coordinating action among lenders.[28] In 1989, then-U.S. Treasury Secretary Nicholas F. Brady proposed what became known as the Brady Plan — a combination of bank loan forgiveness and repackaging remaining debt into bonds that could be traded on securities markets. One key feature of the Brady Plan was for lenders to recognize that doubt over the timely repayment of the existing debt had reduced its value and to agree to allow borrowers to buy back debt at a discount.

After the buyback, the remaining loan principal was restructured using three types of bonds:

> In the first case, dollar-denominated discount bonds paying market interest rates were exchanged for outstanding commercial bank loans. These bonds were interest only; principal was repaid at maturity.

In the second case, dollar-denominated, below market interest rate bonds were exchanged at face (par) value for outstanding commercial bank loans. These bonds, also, were interest only with the principal repaid at maturity.

In the third case, dollar-denominated bonds were exchanged for outstanding loans at face value and paid market interest rates.

In addition, banks provided new money to maintain liquidity of the borrower nations.

Borrower nations were required to purchase U.S. Treasury zero coupon bonds that were held in escrow at the Federal Reserve Bank of New York to partially collateralize the principal of discount and par bonds.[29] Debtor countries, also, collateralized 12-18 months of interest by making a deposit at the Federal Reserve Bank of New York or by purchasing U.S. Treasury bills. The World Bank and the International Monetary Fund (IMF) made structural adjustment loans to debtor nations.

Contemporary Issues

Discussions at the time centered over what countries would be eligible for debt restructuring and the terms of the restructuring. The analogy for aiding homeowners delinquent on mortgage payments would be the question of who should be eligible and how the mortgages should be recast.

Results

The Brady Plan is widely credited with accelerating the creation of new international financing mechanisms. By shifting much lending from bank loans to bonds, liquidity was added to the international financial system, which has grown in the intervening years, benefitting many nations. Liquidity and the multiple types of bond exchanges meant that lenders did not have to agree on a single solution.

Application to Subprime Mortgage Restructuring

On the one hand, the Brady Plan restored financial stability to U.S. commercial banks and international lending grew. More affordable terms and the assurance of long-term financing were benefits to both borrowers and lenders. Brady bonds allowed the federal government to facilitate the restructuring of debt into more affordable payments without any federal guarantee.

On the other hand, shifting the denomination debt from the borrower's currency to dollars shifted exchange rate risk from lenders to borrowers. New collateral shifted more risk from the U.S. banks to the debtor nations. Not every debtor nation was willing and able to renegotiate its loans. Banks negotiated custom agreements with some debtor nations. This was practical because of the size of the loans. Mexico, for example, had $17 billion ($40 billion in 2008 dollars) in short term debt.[30] This renegotiation might be more difficult in the case of two million mortgages that could default in 2008 and 2009, most valued in the hundreds of thousands of dollars.[31]

Lenders recognized losses on existing loans, but had more assurance that renegotiated loans would be repaid in full and on time. Borrowers had more manageable repayment schedules.

A similar approach could be used to restructure subprime loans. Some mortgages could have their principal and/or interest rates reduced. This could be viewed as an acknowledgment of the economic reality that the value of the subprime mortgage is less than its face value because of the weakened value of the home as collateral and the increased probability of default. Lenders might be willing to advance additional funds to some subprime borrowers if these funds were placed in escrow as collateral for a new loan. HOLC used a similar recognition of the reduced value of the mortgages it purchased.

It is likely that not every subprime borrower facing an interest rate reset would be willing or able to renegotiate their loans. Lenders would be unlikely to agree to renegotiate terms that would leave them worse off than foreclosure. For example, if a homeowner cannot afford to make payments on a fixed rate mortgage based on the current value of the home, the lender is likely to decide that foreclosure is the more profitable option. If this inability to make payments is temporary, such as would be the case if someone is unemployed but likely to find a new job shortly, the longer run interests of the lender might be to negotiate a new mortgage. If, however, the inability to make payments is seen as permanent, then lenders are more likely to be unwilling to negotiate.

It is not likely that a domestic private sector, third party would make additional loans to subprime borrowers in a manner such as the IMF and World Bank did for debtor nations. This might be a role for FHA or the Veterans Administration.

CONCLUSION

If Congress were to consider some intervention to aid homeowners, there are a number of questions for its consideration:

Who should be helped? Should there be an income limit? Should it be limited to owner-occupied housing?
What should be the tax treatment of the assistance?
Who should administer the program? What should happen if foreclosure becomes necessary?
What should be the government's continuing role? Should the program have a fixed life?
What restrictions, if any, should be placed on the ability of homeowners that receive assistance to sell their homes in the future? What if the sale is at a profit? What if the sale is at a loss?
If the government makes a financial contribution, how much should it be and how should it be financed?

One of the lessons from these four instances of government intervention is that those in financial difficulty are frequently reluctant to acknowledge the existence or severity of the problem. On the other hand, in these four cases, recognition that substantial losses had occurred was a key to beginning the recovery process. The question remaining was how the losses could be paid for at the least cost.

Most government market interventions have used the emergency medicine principal of triage to divide those into distress into three groups: those who cannot be helped with the resources available, those who will recover (or at least survive) without any help, and those who will recover only with immediate assistance. The difficulty is in determining to which category the affected persons or institutions should be assigned.

HOLC and Brady bonds involved negotiations between the borrower and the organizations involved in the refinancing. Not every distressed borrower was willing or able to meet the terms of the assistance effort. It is probably unrealistic to expect that any plan could keep all subprime borrowers in their homes. For example, some borrowers will become unemployed and not have the income to make even reduced mortgage payments. Even a moratorium on foreclosures would prevent loss of homes only while the moratorium lasts.

The HOLC experience was that some of those who could be helped would not contact the HOLC. It was necessary for HOLC to reach out to borrowers who became delinquent and to develop personalized plans to modify the mortgage so that it could be repaid eventually. Many of the largest mortgage lenders and associations such as those represented by HOPE NOW are urging delinquent homeowners to talk with their lenders and credit counselors.[32] HOPE NOW, also, is dividing callers into three categories trying to work quickly with the easiest situations first so that those who require more extensive help can get the resources needed.

Economists use the phrase "moral hazard" to represent the change in behavior due to insuring risks. Purchasing insurance probably makes some individuals more likely to take risks than would be prudent without the financial safety net. Economists who worry about moral hazard are concerned that a government intervention in a market outcome also encourages individuals and companies to pay less attention to risk in the future in the expectation that the government will intervene again. They worry that in the case of a government intervention to help homeowners, the possibility of a repeat of the intervention could encourage some lenders to lend more than they would, absent the history of government action. It is possible that homeowners who are helped and others who see the intervention occur also could react this way.

REFERENCES

[1] See [http://www.hopenow.com/].

[2] See, for example, Mary Umberger, "Rate freeze called too little, too much; Critics say it delays inevitable; others oppose intervention," *Chicago Tribune*, December 7, 2007, p. 1.

[3] Damian Paletta, "Democrat Floats Plan to Refinance Home Loans With U.S. Help," *Wall Street Journal*, February 27, 2008, p. A14.

[4] Single-family includes structures with one to four units. It excludes condominiums and cooperatives. In 2005, there were 84.5 million owner-occupied single-family buildings, while an additional 7.6 million were vacant. Of those occupied, 67.2 million were occupied by owners and 17.3 million were rentals. Source: U.S. Census Bureau, *American Housing Survey 2005*, Table 1A1, available at [http://www.census.gov/hhes/www/housing/ahs/ahs05/ ahs05 .html].

[5] For details, see CRS Report RL34372, The HOPE NOW Alliance/American Securitization Forum (ASF) Plan to Freeze Certain Mortgage Interest Rates, by David H. Carpenter and Edward Vincent Murphy.

[6] For more details, see the FHA Web page at [http://portal.hud.gov/portal/page?_pageid=33,7 1 7446&_dad=portal&_schema=PORTAL].

[7] CRS Report RL34232, Understanding Mortgage Foreclosure: Recent Events, the Process, and Costs, by Darryl E. Getter. See, also, Amy Crews Cutts and Richard K. Green, Innovative Service Technology: Smart Enough to Keep People in Their Homes, Freddie Mac Working Paper #04-03, July 2004, p. 5, available at [http://www.freddiemac.com/news/pdf/fmwp_0403_servicing.pdf]. (The paper cites a study by Craig Focardi, Servicing Default Management: An Overview of the Process and Underlying Technology," TowerGroup Research Note, No. 033-1 3C, November 15, 2002).

[8] U.S . Congress, Joint Economic Committee, The Subprime Lending Crisis: The Economic Impact on Wealth, Property Values and Tax Revenues, and How We Got Here, October 2007, p. 13 and CRS calculations.

[9] This estimate by GMAC-RFC (Residential Funding Corporation) is cited by Desire Hatcher, "Foreclosure Alternatives: A Case for Preserving Homeownership," *Profitwise News and Views*, February 2006, p. 1, at [http://www.chicagofed.org/community _development/files/02_2006_foreclosure_alt.pdf].

[10] CRS Report RL33930, Subprime Mortgages: Primer on Current Lending and Foreclosure Issues, by Edward Vincent Murphy.

[11] C. Lowell Harriss, *History and Policies of the Home Owners' Loan Corporation* (New York: National Bureau of Economic Research, 1951). 48 Stat. 128 et seq. created the HOLC.

[12] Interest-only payments were later allowed for the first three years. All historic dollar amounts in this report are update to 2008 dollars using the Consumer Price Index and the calculator available from the Federal Reserve Bank of Minneapolis at [http://woodrow.mpls.frb.fed.us/research/data/us/calc/].

[13] This exclusion included estate, inheritance, and gift taxes, but not a progressive surtax.

[14] Harriss, p. 24. money, it ended up ma

[15] Harriss, p. 6.

[16] Harriss, p. 75.

[17] Harriss, p. 75.

[18] Harriss, p. 140.

[19] In a time when all records were kept on paper, a bank failure could prevent homeowners from making mortgage payments resulting in their delinquency.

[20] Federal Deposit Insurance Corporation, "Continental Illinois and Too Big To Fail" and "Continental Illinois National Bank and Trust Company," *History of the Eighties — Lessons for the Future*, at [http://www.fdic.gov/bank/historical/history/235_258.pdf#search=' Continental%20Illinois'] and [http : //www.fdic . gov/bank/historical/ managing/ history2-04.pdf], respectively. A "money center bank" is one of the nation's largest and usually does business internationally with governments, businesses, and other banks.

[21] P.L. 102-242, 105 Stat. 2236 et seq.

[22] See CRS Report RL34420, Bear Stearns: Crisis and 'Rescue' for a Major Provider of Mortgage-Related Products, by Gary Shorter.

[23] In short, the S&Ls financed long term loans by taking in short term deposits. When interest rates increased, to keep and to attract deposits the S&Ls had to pay higher interest rates than they were earning on their loans.

[24] P.L. 101-73, 103 Stat. 183 et seq.

[25] Timothy Curry and Lynn Shibut, "The Cost of the Savings and Loan Crisis: Truth and Consequences," FDIC Banking Review, December 2000, p. 31, available at [http://www.fdic.gov/bank/ analytical/banking/ 2000dec/brv1 3n2_2.pdf].

[26] P.L. 96-22 1, 94 Stat. 132 et seq., Depository Institutions Deregulation and Monetary Control Act of 1980.

[27] This section is based on CRS Report RL30348, *Ecuador's Brady Bond Default: Background and Implications*, by J. F. Hornbeck, and also Patricia A. Wertman, "The 'Brady Plan': A New Director in Third World Debt Strategy," *CRS Review*, October 1989, pp. 22-23.

[28] Mark Spiegel, "Collective Action Difficulties in Foreign Lending: Banks and Bonds," *Federal Reserve Bank of San Francisco Economic Letter*, August 23, 1996, available at [http://www.frbsf.org/econrsrch/ wklyltr/el9 6-24.html].

[29] The issuer of a zero coupon bond pays all interest and principal at maturity. The bond is sold for less than this single payment. A zero coupon bond pays compound interest — interest on interest like a saving account does — while a coupon bond pays simple interest.

[30] "Companies and Markets: Focus on Precise Terms of Mexican Debt Moratorium," *Financial Times*, August 31, 1982, p. 19.

[31] Mark Zandi, "Testimony of Mark Zandi before U.S. House Judiciary Committee," October 30, 2007, at [http://judiciary.house.gov/Oversight Testimony.aspx?ID=1 188].

[32] Members of HOPE NOW include Fannie Mae, Freddie Mac, Bank of America, Countrywide, JPMorgan Chase, Washington Mutual, and Wells Fargo. A complete list is available at [http://www.hopenow.com/]. In addition, FHA is urging borrowers experiencing financial difficulty to contact their lenders. FHA has information available at [http://portal.hud.gov/portal/page?_pageid=33,7 17348&_dad =portal&_schema=PORTAL].

In: Understanding Mortgage Meltdowns
Editor: A. V. Carey
ISBN: 978-1-60692-789-2

Chapter 8

PROPOSAL TO ALLOW TREASURY TO BUY MORTGAGE-RELATED ASSETS TO ADDRESS FINANCIAL INSTABILITY*

Edward V. Murphy and Baird Webel

ABSTRACT

Financial markets underwent severe stress during the week of September 15-22, 2008. After Lehman Brothers declared bankruptcy and AIG received a bridge loan from the Federal Reserve, policymakers reassessed their case-by-case approach to resolving financial problems. Secretary of the Treasury Paulson announced a plan to allow Treasury to purchase mortgage-related assets from U.S. financial institutions. The announced intent of the plan is to unclog financial markets, increase the health of the banking sector, and reduce ongoing risks to the economy. This report discusses a draft of the proposal as it stood on September 21, 2008, and analyzes frequently asked questions. This report will be updated as conditions warrant.

Following a week of severe stress in financial markets, the Secretary of the Treasury and the Chairman of the Federal Reserve met with congressional leaders on September 19, 2008, to ask for legislation to authorize direct intervention in the economy. An unofficial three-page draft of a specific proposal circulated over the weekend of September 20, 2008.[1] A revised draft circulated September 21.

* Excerpted from CRS Report RS22957, dated September 22, 2008.

Both draft proposals allow Treasury to purchase up to $700 billion in mortgage-related assets in an attempt to reduce disruptions in the financial system. This report describes the provisions of the draft legislative proposals that were circulated and provides an analysis of several questions that the proposals raise.

The Draft Proposals

Purchase of Mortgage-Related Assets

The proposal grants Treasury the authority to purchase mortgage-related assets for two years. The proposal would limit the amount of assets purchased to $700 billion outstanding at any one time. Funding for the purchases comes from selling Treasury securities. The Secretary of the Treasury is granted discretion to administer the program, and decisions by the Secretary would not be reviewable in court or by any administrative agency.

Debt Limit

Both draft proposals increase the debt limit of the federal government. The new debt limit in each draft is $11,315,000,000,000. This $11.3 trillion new limit compares to the current debt limit of $10.6 trillion. The total current debt is $9.6 trillion. If the full authority of the program were immediately exercised and funded exclusively with new debt, and there were no additional new debt from existing government operations, the current debt would rise to $10.3 trillion.

Definition of Troubled Asset

The September 20 draft defines mortgage-related assets as "residential or commercial mortgages and any securities, obligations, or other instruments that are based on or related to such mortgages, that in each case was issued on or before September 17, 2008."

The September 21 draft defines troubled assets in the same way but adds a clause allowing the Secretary of the Treasury in consultation with the Chairman of the

Federal Reserve to add any other financial instrument, "the purchase of which the Secretary determines necessary to promote financial market stability."

These definitions could encompass whole mortgage loans, mortgage-backed securities (MBS), and subordinated mortgage securities such as collateralized debt obligations (CDOs) or collateralized mortgage obligations (CMOs). It is unclear whether the September 20 definition also encompasses derivatives that reference the defaults of underlying mortgages in MBS such as certain credit default swaps (CD S). The September 21 draft would allow the purchase of credit default swaps if the Chairman of the Federal Reserve agreed. It is unclear whether the Secretary of the Treasury could purchase CDS without Federal Reserve consultation under the September 21 language.

Authority to Take Action

Using the term "necessary actions," the draft proposals grant authority to administer the program and place certain limits on participation. Treasury may employ personnel, contract for services, and issue appropriate definitions, regulations, and guidances. Treasury may designate financial institutions as financial agents of the government. Treasury may also establish vehicles authorized to purchase mortgage-related assets and issue obligations. The administrative vehicles could encompass trusts or corporations to administer the assets. The September 21 draft also includes a provision to apply Federal Acquisition Regulation when awarding contracts to asset managers and requires the asset managers to acknowledge a fiduciary duty to the United States.

Restrictions

The draft proposals include two significant restrictions. First, purchased assets must have been originated or issued before September 17, 2008. Furthermore, the seller of the asset to the Treasury is limited to "any financial institution having its headquarters in the United States." Under the September 20 draft proposal, it is unclear whether U.S. affiliates of foreign institutions would be included. Similarly, it is unclear whether there are restrictions on the ability of U.S. institutions to serve as intermediaries, buying mortgage assets from foreign institutions and then selling them to Treasury.

Under the September 21 draft proposal, foreign central banks and institutions owned by foreign governments are specifically excluded. This draft directs the

Treasury to coordinate with foreign financial authorities to work to establish similar authorities overseas and to coordinate activities.

Factors to Guide Intervention

The draft proposals listed two factors for Treasury to consider when exercising authority under the program. First, Treasury shall consider means for "providing stability or preventing disruption to the financial markets or banking system." The proposal does not provide a definition for the terms stability, disruption, financial market, or banking system. Second, Treasury shall consider means for "protecting the taxpayer." Protection is not defined.

Management of Mortgage-Related Assets

Treasury is given authority to manage the mortgage-related assets acquired through the program. Management includes exercising any rights acquired through purchase (presumably including any rights regarding foreclosure in the case of whole loans). Rights of management of assets acquired before the termination of the program extends beyond the termination date; that is, Treasury can continue to hold acquired mortgage assets after the expiration of authority to acquire new mortgage-related assets. Treasury may also manage the mortgage revenues and any portfolio risk of the program.

Loss Mitigation and Loan Modification

The September 20 draft did not contain any provisions for loss mitigation or loan modification of mortgage loans. The September 21 draft contains two provisions to address troubled borrowers. First, for whole mortgage loans acquired by Treasury, loan servicers must follow industry best practices for loan modifications. Best practices are identified by the Secretary in consultation with the Hope for Homeowners Oversight Board. Second, if the program acquires MBS or similar assets that put the government in the position of one of the investors with an interest in an underlying mortgage, then the government will consent to reasonable loan modifications.

Sunset

Authority to purchase mortgage-related assets under the program expires two years from the date of enactment. Recall that authority to manage already acquired mortgage-related assets continues after the sunset provision.

Reports to Congress

The Secretary of the Treasury must report to congressional committees with respect to authority exercised under the program. The first report is required within three months of first exercise of authority, and reports continue semiannually thereafter. The committees to report to include the Committee on the Budget, Financial Services, and Ways and Means of the House of Representatives and the Committees on the Budget, Finance, and Banking, Housing, and Urban Affairs of the Senate. The September 21 draft also requires a GAO study on the impact of troubled asset purchases.

Frequently Asked Questions

Does the proposal include provisions to help home owners facing foreclosure?

The September 20 draft proposal did not include any provisions specifically designed to help home owners facing foreclosure. The September 21 draft requires loan servicers to follow industry best practices and to modify loans in accordance with the Hope for Homeowners Oversight Board.

Proponents of such measures might argue that actions to unfreeze mortgage markets will help liquidity flow back into mortgage markets, which in turn might make it easier for borrowers to refinance out of troubled mortgages or sell their homes to avoid foreclosure. Critics might counter that this is a relatively expensive and indirect way to aid troubled mortgage borrowers.

Is the program limited to home mortgages?

No. The program also includes securities based on residential mortgages. It is unclear whether the program applies to derivatives that reference mortgage-related securities. In addition to residential mortgages, the draft proposals also include commercial mortgages and related assets.

What price will Treasury pay for the assets it purchases?

The proposal leaves the price to the discretion of the Secretary of the Treasury. A press release states that the price of assets purchased will be established through market mechanisms where possible, such as through reverse auctions.[2]

What happens to funds the Treasury receives from disposing of the assets?

Treasury's press release reports that returns from the sale of assets will be returned to Treasury's general fund for the benefit of taxpayers.

What is the potential cost of bad mortgage-related debt?

The answer to this question depends in large part on real estate markets. On the residential side, if house prices continue to decline, then the number of home owners who cannot sell or refinance to avoid foreclosure will continue to rise. The performance of commercial mortgages going forward will be affected by developments in the broader economy. If a deep recession is avoided, then commercial mortgage defaults may be minimized.

The program appears to be targeted at the troubled mortgage-related assets that are burdening bank balance sheets. If this is the case, then certain categories of securities may be more likely to be acquired than others. For example, because of the explicit Treasury guarantees associated with the conservatorship of Fannie Mae and Freddie Mac, their securities (called agency debt and agency MBS) should be of less immediate concern. This suggests that the problem assets are more likely to be in the non-agency sector. According to one industry source,[3] the estimate of outstanding non-agency MBS was $1.3 trillion at the end of 2007, with another $25 billion issued in 2008. There was also another $1.3 trillion in outstanding collateralized mortgage obligations. Thus, the total amount of mortgage-related assets that might be acquired by the program would be nearly four times the $700 billion limit in the proposal.

The above estimate does not include any direct purchases of whole mortgage loans or derivatives that reference the mortgage-related assets. However, it might be double counting to include both the mortgage-related securities and the underlying mortgages or referenced derivatives. If issues with the underlying mortgages are resolved, then any mortgage-backed security or derivative that references those mortgages would not be in default.

What role did housing play in financial turmoil?

Several factors have contributed to financial instability, but most observers agree that a major component of the financial stress has been the boom and bust in housing that coincided with low short- term interest rates. It has been argued that rapid house price appreciation in some areas and low interest rates led to overconfidence by investors, lenders, borrowers, and regulators. Builders responded to higher prices with increased construction, and the pace of home price increases could not be sustained. Inventories of unsold homes began climbing and prices stagnated at the same time as short-term interest rates began rising. Any borrowers, including in the subprime market, who had depended on being able to refinance at low interest rates or depended on rapid home price appreciation found their plans frustrated and defaults occurred at increasing rates. The value of financial assets that depended on home owners making their payments, such as mortgage-backed securities (MBS), declined significantly.

How did financial markets magnify the effects of mortgage defaults?

Three factors in the financial system magnified the effects of defaults by reducing confidence, particularly in bank balance sheets.

Lack of transparency — The financial structures used to fund mortgages had become very complex, making it harder for firms to assess the value of assets or the condition of potential counterparties.

Leverage — Because financial firms had very little capital relative to their commitments, even small percentage declines in the value of their mortgage assets could significantly impair their solvency. Combined with poor transparency, this further contributed to caution on the part of counterparties in financial transactions.

Derivatives — Increased use of complex derivatives, such as credit default swaps, made it very difficult to project how the failure of a financial firm would affect other firms. Would counterparties to derivatives contracts have the reserves to fulfill their obligations? If not, would the marking down of derivative values cause a new round of de-leveraging?

How, if at all, could financial turmoil affect the wider economy if nothing is done?

There are several sectors of the economy that depend on regular financing to operate. Also, consumers frequently depend on financing to purchase expensive items. Therefore, disruptions to the financial system can cause problems for business investment and consumer expenditures on durable goods. In addition, declines in the value of assets linked to finance, such as houses and retirement accounts, cause consumers to feel poorer and to cut back spending.

How, if at all, could intervention in mortgage-related securities markets calm financial markets?

An intervention in financial markets could restore financial stability if it restores confidence. Removing bad debt from bank balance sheets directly addresses several problems. Shortcomings in transparency become a less pressing concern for institutions that can participate because counterparties would know that the institution has the opportunity to clean up its balance sheet. Similarly, the program may provide an orderly way to resolve derivatives contracts.

What is the rationale for acting now?

According to a press release from the Treasury, illiquid mortgage-related assets had clogged the financial system.[4] The juxtaposition of the refusal to intervene on behalf of Lehman Brothers the same week that a bridge loan was extended to AIG has convinced some that the case-by-case approach of recent weeks should be replaced by a more broadly based intervention. In addition, the sudden spike in interest rate spreads and declines in financial activity following the AIG intervention convinced some policymakers that financial fragilities could worsen if they are not addressed.

How did interest rate spreads indicate a sudden loss of confidence?

"Spreads" often refers to the difference between a particular interest rate and the yield of a Treasury security of comparable maturity (although there are other spreads). So defined, high spreads are often an indicator that people believe the Treasury security to be less risky than the other asset (although there can be other reasons for widening spreads.) Although the Federal Reserve had lowered policy interest rates to 2% by April 2008, other interest rates remained relatively high. Examples include the interest rate that banks charge each other, the interest rate on asset-backed commercial paper, and mortgage rates. The Federal Housing Finance Agency (FHFA) indicated that the high spreads on Fannie and Freddie securities were a significant factor in the decision to put the companies into conservatorship. Then, during the week of September 15-20, following the Lehman Brothers bankruptcy and the loan to AIG, the spread on commercial paper almost tripled in a single day, and prompting concern that the entire financial system could shut down.

Couldn't the same assets be purchased through Fannie Mae and Freddie Mac now that they are in a conservatorship backed by the Treasury?

Only parts of the proposal could be implemented through Fannie Mae and Freddie Mac. First, the charters of Fannie Mae and Freddie Mac do not allow them to acquire commercial mortgages. Second, some of the delinquent mortgages that contribute to the problem are jumbo loans in California (jumbo refers to mortgages too large to be purchased by Fannie Mae and Freddie Mac). However, Fannie Mae and Freddie Mac could acquire residential MBS that conform to their new higher loan limits. Operating a troubled MBS and mortgage purchase program through Fannie Mae and Freddie Mac would have a similar result as under the new proposal because Treasury is already committed to purchase preferred stock to maintain the solvency of the institutions.

REFERENCES

[1] This report is based on a draft acquired via email from CongressNow Alert. "Alert: Bush Administration Financial Plan," *CongressNow*, September 20, 2008, 10:21 a.m. CongressNow is a Roll Call Group Business and distributed the alert through emails@congressnow.com.

[2] "Statement by Secretary Henry M. Paulson, Jr. on Comprehensive Approach to Market Developments," Press Release, Department of Treasury, September 19, 2008, available at [http://www.treas.gov/press/releases/hp 11 49.htm].

[3] Statistics from the Securities Industry and Financial Markets Association (SIFMA), available at [http://www.sifma.org/research/statistics/market-sector-statistics.shtml#mbs].

[4] "Statement by Secretary Henry M. Paulson, Jr. on Comprehensive Approach to Market Developments," Press Release, Department of Treasury, September 19, 2008, available at [http://www.treas.gov/press/releases/hp 11 49.htm].

INDEX

A

B

D

G

H

I

S

W

Y

Z